commit to confidence

30 strategies to help women step up and stand out

barbara roche

Lois —
Confidence
makes the
outfit!

ISBN - 978-1-105-92854-3

acknowledgments

There's an old saying that behind every successful woman are a lot of other women. I could not have said it better. This book is dedicated to my coaching clients who have taught me more about confidence than I could have ever learned on my own. And of course, special thanks go to my sisters, cousins, and dear friends. I would not have completed this book without you – especially Mare and Claire. Finally, thank you to my husband Michael, who after weeks of watching me road-test possible book titles that ultimately went splat, came bounding up the stairs yelling, "OK! I've got it! Commit to Confidence, because unless you commit to something you will never make it happen."

"Girls will be your friends...but just remember, some come, some go.
The ones that stay with you through everything – they're your
true best friends. Don't let go of them. Also remember,
sisters make the best friends in the world."

- Marilyn Monroe

table of contents

introduction

Imagine you are competing at the Olympic Games. You are a vital member of a team that will become known as the Magnificent Seven, but you don't know that yet. All you know is that the chance to win Gold has come down to the final round of the final event, and *you* are the final competitor.

On the first attempt to hurl yourself over the vault in an explosive yet oh so graceful manner, you seriously injure your ankle. And now, on top of having to overcome all the fear and doubt that comes with Olympic-level competition, you sense your determination is wavering because you can't stop thinking about your ankle and the inevitable crippling pain that will likely shoot up your leg on the first step. The other thought in your head is just as strong: there is no room for error. Even the slightest mistake could cost your team the Gold medal.

As you stare down the 80-foot runway, the doubting voices grow louder, and that's when you see your coach walking toward you. You turn to him – the world famous Bela Karolyi who has already led Nadia and Mary Lou to gold medals and Wheaties boxes – and you ask, "Do we need this?" There it is. The voice in your head telling you that you can't do it, you shouldn't do it, you-are-crazy-for-even-thinking about doing it comes spilling out in that one question. Your coach grips you by the shoulders, looks right in your eyes, and says in his thick, Hungarian accent, "You ken doit Keddi. One more time. You kendoit!"

At that point you turn back to the runway, raise your hand to signal the judges and off you go, barreling down the runway at 13 miles per hour. You hit the springboard with full force, then your hands magically hit the vault and you catapult yourself into the air like the eraser side of a pencil hitting the floor. You soar high in the air as your body flips and twists with catlike reflexes. And now, the holy grail, as your feet turn toward the ground you contort your body into an aerodynamic shape that helps you stick the landing. Bam! The crowd goes wild as you lift your re-injured ankle off the floor with one arm, and perform your final "tada" for the judges with the other.

Because of your commitment to confidence, your team wins its first team gold.

It was at this moment in 1996, when Kerri Strug performed her final vault, I started thinking seriously about the word confidence – the shoulders back, head up, bring it on kind of daring that comes from knowing our own strengths and letting go of the limiting beliefs that may start out as a slight hesitation or minor second-guessing, but can easily lead to crippling self-doubt. At the time, it was because I was itching for a more substantial leadership position. Some part of me was hesitant, but after watching the Magnificent Seven, I told myself to get moving.

Fast-forward 15 years and a transition to running my own coaching and consulting practice, I found myself having a conversation with a colleague about my next goal in life, which was to write this book. She asked me to sum it up in one sentence. That stopped me in my tracks. What *was* the point of this book? Thinking long and hard about the 'who, what, and why' of my goal, I finally got back to her and said, "The purpose of this book is to help women make a conscious decision to *act* from a place of confidence rather than to *ask* from a place of uncertainty."

This book is my attempt to capture all the Aha! moments I have had as an executive coach working with professional women in a wide range of industries and job titles, and as a professor of leadership communication at the undergraduate and graduate level. In the early days of my coaching career, I would feel a twinge of sadness when I heard a smart and talented woman question her own capabilities, even in the face of actual data proving otherwise. Now I see it as an emotional poison that must be eradicated.

I remember being in a coaching session with a talented, attractive and successful woman who was dealing with a particularly thorny issue at work when she said, "I'm not smart enough to handle this on my own. What if I make a mistake?" On my drive home I began seriously considering the prospects of freeing the female brain from the "I'm not [fill in the blank] enough" mindset. To put it in the words of one of my clients, "It's as if women come with an automatic apology for any and all of our perceived inadequacies." I got stuck on the idea that there had to be a way to cancel out those negative voices. I realized right then I could do something about it. I could start chipping away at the behemoth of low self-esteem with each page of this book.

Without having to search very far, I was able to validate my hypothesis that there is a direct correlation between a woman's lack of confidence and the low number of female CEOs in this country.[1] A recent study by McKinsey & Co. found the majority of women allowed self-limiting beliefs to hold them back, either by feeling they should wait to be asked to apply for a promotion, or feeling they lacked the skills and abilities to perform in a more demanding role.[2] It would be convenient to chalk it up to factors like having less testosterone or striving for a balance between work and family. In reality, it's less about our X chromosome and more about the messages we internalize and how those messages impact our ability to feel confident and capable. I will share a recent example to illustrate my point.

During a leadership development workshop, I asked the participants to think of a time when they were effective and powerful – when they felt the most energized and proud of an outcome they had a hand in creating. I then asked them to share their story with a partner. Within seconds, the room was alive with voices and laughter, and I thought to myself, "I'm so lucky I get to do this for a living!" As I was walking around the room, I noticed one participant raise her hand. When I approached, she asked, "What if you can't think of anything?"

For a brief moment, I was dumbstruck. I had a hard time wrapping my head around the fact that a person over the age of 18 could not come up with one example of personal efficacy. I had a sudden notion she may not be alone in her struggle and that other women in the room might be undermining their own accomplishments, so I asked her if I could share her question with the whole group. She agreed.

When I re-convened the group, I asked the participant to repeat the question, after which there was a collective sigh. I then asked her a series of questions with the help of the audience, and we uncovered the fact that she was an owner of a small construction company with 40 employees and several new contracts. Pretty impressive. I then asked her where in that entire description of a successful business owner could she not identify a peak moment. And her response captures the impetus for this book. She said, "I just figure that's what everybody does and so it's nothing to be particularly proud of."

Later that day, I thought about why this particular woman chose to hide her light under a bushel. Minimizing success often results in a depleted supply of self-confidence. Successful people use their accomplishments as confidence-builders. Yet many women view them as just another day; as items on a never-ending *To Do* list that must be completed so we can move onto another task. With that mindset, we simply lose out on the compound interest we could be accruing. Confidence has a spillover effect that makes life so much fuller. It's the difference between the movie screen in a 20-seat theatre and an I-Max.

Confidence is directly linked to our sense of competence, to a belief in our own capabilities. When we are in full "can-do" mode, we are better able to tame the triple demons of fear, doubt and insecurity, and suddenly, stepping out of our comfort zone doesn't seem so scary.

Confidence is powerful. It's sexy. More goals are achieved through confidence in oneself than by stressing over supposed inadequacies. The world would be a better place if rather than shying away from opportunity because it feels too scary, we instead just took the leap and asserted our opinions and ideas. Advance the ball. Make things happen. Instigate success.

This book is organized around five areas in which women tend to experience a crisis of confidence:

1. cultivating personal presence (what if nobody likes me?)
2. landing your dream job (what if I'm not talented enough?)
3. speaking in public (what if I forget what I'm going to say?)
4. persuading others (what if no one listens to me?)
5. enhancing your personal brand (what if I'm not very interesting?)

Sprinkled throughout the book are mini-coaching sessions designed to help you gain a deeper awareness of your capabilities and with each session, to feel an immediate sense of possibility. Feel free to throw the book down, go out and do something you've been hesitating to do, and then come back to the next section.

I hope this book helps you loosen the restraints around your personal efficacy and remove the barriers keeping you from taking considerable action to achieve your goals. No more waiting for the right time. No more hesitation. No more busy work to distract from doing the scary thing. Running in place certainly gives the impression of activity, but it is simply a more vigorous form of waiting. To my knowledge, it has never helped anyone win a race.

One more thing before we start. You will notice during some of the coaching sessions that I ask you to say your answers out loud. After the second or third time you see this request you might start to wonder if I've lost my short term memory. I promise there is a method to my madness, and it's this: every time one of my female clients has a breakthrough in feeling more competent or gets clear about what's holding her back she says, "Wow, I can't believe I just said that out loud!"

It seems fitting to end this introduction with a quote from one of the most confident and successful women of the last century, who said a lot of things out loud.

"You only live once,

but if you do it right,

once is enough."

- Mae West

chapter 1: cultivating personal presence

"When I walk into a networking event I get so freaked out
that every part of me wants to run the other way.
What I do instead is look down at my iPhone."

- Jane, in the midst of a job search

A few years ago I booked a lunch meeting with a successful CEO to convince him I was the person he should hire to coach members of his leadership team. When we talked by phone to schedule the meeting, he admitted he would probably sign up for a few sessions because he was having trouble getting buy-in and commitment from his team. Suddenly the confidence I was feeling only moments ago was dissipating and quickly being replaced by a growing anxiety. I had not anticipated becoming his coach. What if he wasn't all that impressed? I thought about cancelling the meeting, but what kind of coach would I be then?

As soon as we sat down he began regaling me with his career accomplishments. As he talked (and talked), I kept noticing that he was ignoring every attempt the waitress made to take our order. He barely looked in her direction. Even when she finally stood at our table, he gave her a "talk to the hand" gesture indicating she should stand there and wait for him to finish talking. At first I thought he was oblivious to his bad manners, but by the end of the meal I realized that his overblown sense of entitlement was causing him to be intentionally dismissive of those around him, including me. Could I assume he behaved the same way at work? Of course I could. This was a leader who lacked presence.

Personal presence may be as hard to define as the criteria for winning the disco-ball trophy on *Dancing With The Stars*, but there are a few key elements that are indisputable. Before we get into those elements, let's clear up the myths. Personal presence is not defined by your height, shoulder width, the squareness of your jaw, or your

Louis Vuitton handbag. And just because you never played a varsity sport or you sometimes feel insecure does not mean you will forever lack presence.

It is, however, characterized by who shows up – the attentive listener with a relaxed readiness and a clear sense of her own worth; or the preoccupied, empty vessel with tense energy who is too distracted to make any meaningful connection.

In a word, personal presence comes down to energy. Have you ever been part of a lively discussion? How about a concert by your favorite band or an all tied-up in the ninth inning World Series game? How did you feel? Most likely you felt attentive, fully focused, and the time flew by. A great feeling, right? Imagine people feeling that way about you. If you look up the word "lively" in the dictionary, you find it has several attributes:

1. Full of energy, zest or vigor
2. Quick and energetic
3. Elastic; rebounds readily
4. Filled with events or activity
5. Full of spirit
6. Characterized by energetic activity

Dynamic and successful people have energy. This does not mean everyone has to be a perky cheerleader with a perpetually sunny personality. On the contrary, many successful people have a quiet energy, a discernible low hum that can attract the interest of others just as easily as the louder, more expressive styles. The point is successful people bring this calmly confident energy to work every day. Not because they *can*, but because they *care*.

Now let's look at a few of the strategies you can apply to develop or enhance your personal presence.

Your Mother was Right – You Should Stand up Straight!

If you're like me, you enjoy watching the TV show *What Not to Wear* with Stacy London and Clinton Kelly. They both have presence that comes through the screen and great chemistry with each other. Some of the "reveals" are transformational. Yet in the final scene, when the participant comes out from the darkened room and walks toward the mirror with the new clothes, hairstyle and Carmindized face, she will still have the same hunched posture and sluggish gait she started with. A *complete* makeover would have these women standing tall with their head high and walking with determination.

I remember working with a mid-level manager in a large company who was preparing for a big presentation. This was during the second or third season of *American Idol*, and when I asked her what she would like from me in the way of feedback, she said, "I don't want Paula Abdul, I want Simon Cowell." OK, then!

After the first run-through, I decided to honor her request and said: "When you slouch like that you add ten years to your age and you look unsure of yourself." That got her attention. We watched it back on videotape and afterwards she said, "Wow! No one has ever said that to me before, but it's plainly obvious on the video clip. No wonder I'm having trouble getting promoted."

It's quite possible her reaction was legitimate. At the same time, it's highly unlikely poor posture was the only barrier to a promotion. Given the fact that personal presence is such an important factor in career advancement, I accepted her conclusion. We began working on all aspects of her body language and delivery style so she would not only feel confident during her presentation, but she would have a greater impact on her audience.

Researchers Dana Carney and Amy Cuddy conducted experiments to prove humans can express power by using good posture, and conversely, express powerlessness with bad posture. In their words, "high-power posers experienced elevations in testosterone, decreases in cortisol, and increased feelings of power and tolerance for risk; low-power posers exhibited the opposite pattern. In short, these findings suggest embodiment extends beyond mere thinking and feeling, to physiology and subsequent behavioral choices. That a person can, by assuming [certain] poses, instantly become more powerful has real-world, actionable implications."[3]

The researchers are referring to the basic superhero pose – the kind of pose that takes up space: wide stance, shoulders back, lifted torso, chin level with the ground. Most of my female students tend to do the opposite by taking up the least amount of space, especially when they feel nervous or self-conscious. Feet crossed, shoulders forward and chin lowered; sending all the wrong signals.

The posture research has significant implications for anyone who has to really impress their audience. Adopting a tall, confident posture doesn't just make you feel better emotionally, it makes you feel more powerful biochemically – increasing your testosterone and decreasing your cortisol (or stress hormone). Our mothers always knew that posture was important, but it's nice to see quality research that proves it. The next time you are feeling less than confident, strike a high power pose. That is, take up more space. Stay like that for two minutes, and you might experience what Carney and Cuddy have found in their research, which is that our bodies can change our minds, our minds can change our behavior, and our behavior can change the outcome.

Is good posture only achievable by those who started taking ballet lessons at age seven? Fortunately, the answer is no. So, what *are* the elements of good posture? The National Posture Institute has the answer. They offer four points of posture with simple cues that can lead to better postural alignment. Take a moment to grade yourself on these elements:

- ☐ **Stand Tall:** Visualize the vertebral column lengthening and growing taller

- ☐ **Hold Chest High:** Visualize opening up the chest and creating a 90° angle of the neck and shoulders by leveling out the shoulders

- ☐ **Retract Scapulae:** Visualize holding a pencil between the shoulder blades

- ☐ **Contract Abdominals:** Visualize drawing the navel toward the spine and contracting the core muscles.

www.npionline.org

When I coach women, I include a few more tips:

- ☐ Don't lock your knees (the main cause of fainting in public!).

- ☐ Avoid wearing heels so high that your hips and lower back pitch forward.

- ☐ Avoid sitting into one hip. Keep your weight balanced on both feet.

Next time you need to get your point across – whether you are standing or sitting; whether you are talking to two people or 200 – take a moment to lengthen your spine, lift your rib cage, bring your chin to a neutral position (not up or down, but parallel to the floor) and rotate your shoulders back and down. Plant your feet shoulder-width apart (or if sitting, firmly planted on the floor) and you are ready to make a great impression.

You may have set a New Year's Resolution to advance your career or maybe even find a life partner. If you are reading this in the middle of May, it's still a great time to set an intention to increase your confidence. Posture is one of the necessary (and easily accessible) elements to achieving that goal.

Your Word Choices Can Undermine Your Poker Face

Have you ever heard of the red car syndrome? You buy a red car and then suddenly, all you see on the highway are red cars? That's what happened to me after reading Malcolm Gladwell's book *Outliers* in which he focuses on a concept known as "mitigated speech," a term coined by linguists to describe deferential speech inherent in communication between individuals of perceived power differential (such as boss and subordinate). Gladwell describes it as "any attempt to downplay or sugarcoat the meaning of what is being said." [4] In my experience as an executive coach and professor, I find women use mitigating speech more often than men.

Since my tenure began at the Wharton School in 2008, the number of females accepted into the MBA program has grown to a promising 42 percent. That's the good news. The bad news is that I often notice the mitigated speech patterns that are noticeably different from the way their male counterparts speak. A few of the more common examples are:

> I think
> Maybe
> Somewhat
> Sort of

And a few of the more damaging examples:

> I had a *lot* of help
> It's not that impressive
> It's no big deal
> Never mind

Imagine if Shakespeare had used mitigated speech in Julius Caesar. Instead of Mark Antony's famous and powerful opener, "Friends, Romans, countrymen, lend me your ears..." it would have been, "Friends, Romans, countrymen...is this a bad time?" The power and conviction are gone and what's left is a soup sandwich.

Why do women do this more than men? Why do we minimize our own power and sometimes even forfeit our place at the table? For the purposes of this book, let's focus on one possible reason: we are approval-seekers; we are people-pleasers. We think the way to get along is to go along. Reality TV notwithstanding, we're told that *nice* is more important than *decisive*; "pretty in pink" will get us a husband, and "badass in black" will just get us, well, let's move on. These belief systems mean that we can trip ourselves up along the way without even noticing we've stumbled. Then suddenly, we wonder why our male counterpart is getting paid $5,000 more for the same job with the same qualifications.

There is even more compelling evidence proving the negative impact of mitigated speech. James Pennebaker at the University of Texas at Austin has conducted research on our word choices, specifically the difference between "content" words – nouns, adjectives, verbs – which reveal less about an individual's personality or state of mind than "function" words. Function words are the pronouns and prepositions in a sentence. The clearest examples are "and" and "but." Others are if, my, I, with, have, for, he, she, of, and on.[5]

In his new book, *The Secret Life of Pronouns: What our Words Say About Us*, Pennebaker explains that there are about 500 function words in the English language and 150 of them are the most common. He says function words "help shape and shortcut language." While they only comprise .5% of the entire English dictionary, they account for 55% of what we speak, hear and read (hbr.org, 2012).

Here are just a few of Pennebaker's findings:

- A depressed person uses "I" more often than a happy person
- People who are lying use no, none, and never more frequently
- Couples who use similar language tend to stay together longer
- We don't hear the function words we use in conversation

What does this mean for boosting confidence and getting the results we want? Our choice of pronouns can help us telegraph how we are feeling inside. When we realize that our doubts and fears are being telegraphed no matter how hard we are trying to hide them, we might be more apt to banish the negative voice when it tiptoes into the room.

Stop Your "Backstory" Before it Stops You

I was meeting with a client the other day to help her rehearse an upcoming presentation. We'll call her Rhonda. She explained how critical this presentation was to her career. She was to present a new venture to the Board of Directors that would require a significant investment in time, staff hours, and money, but would also help the company grow market share if the project was a success. Clearly the stakes were high, and her role in the organization would either be significantly enhanced – possibly even result in a promotion – or be diminished to the point where she would not get another opportunity in a very long time.

After walking me through the content and the mechanics of the Board meeting, Rhonda stood up and delivered the presentation from start to finish. I noticed that her presentation style leaned toward the dry side; factual, declarative, and flat. Imagine asking your sweetheart, "Honey, do you love me?" And the response was, "I told you I loved you when I married you and nothing has changed." Now you get the picture.

We then sat down to discuss ways to enhance the presentation and things she could do to be more influential. Here's the gist of the conversation:

Me: "Can you find a way to be more animated in your delivery so your excitement about the project comes across to your audience?"

Rhonda: "No way. I can't do exuberant. I'm not a very animated person."

Me: "Sure you are. You just showed me."

Rhonda: *(aghast)* "When?!"

Me: "Thirty minutes ago when you told me about your son making the traveling soccer team."

Rhonda: "Oh, well, that's different. I could talk about him for hours. What you're asking me to do is very different. I don't know how to be full of life on command."

Me: "You're thinking about Lady Macbeth and I'm thinking about authenticity. If the Board doesn't sense your faith in the project then why should they approve it? They're going to need a reason to vote yes and facts alone won't do the trick."

Rhonda: "So you're saying if I bring the same kind of energy to the presentation I just showed when talking about my son, I will make a stronger impact on the Board."

Me: "Only if you truly feel that way about the project."

Rhonda: "I do!"

Me: "Then can you make sure they know that?"

Rhonda: "Definitely. Let's try it again!"

What made this otherwise smart and successful person go through her adult life thinking she was unable to be a dynamic communicator? The likely culprit is what Deepak Chopra calls our emotional "backstory."[6] Backstories emerge out of our childhood and adolescent memories. We create stories out of these memories and the negative ones become "full of hostility and resentment." Then we carry these stories with us every day and they emerge during high-stress or pressurized moments and sabotage our success.

As Rhonda told me afterward, the smartest thing she did was take the time to practice her presentation and get meaningful feedback.

Without it, she would have presented her case in an unconvincing manner all because she believed her personality tended toward the unenthusiastic.

Chopra goes on to say that the most amazing thing about human beings is we can find a way to tell ourselves a *new* story. He suggests starting with this question: "Is this really true?" Then ask, "Who would I be if the other story were true?" In Rhonda's case, she started to reorient around the idea that she could actually be more animated and show genuine enthusiasm for something she truly cared about.

I'm happy to report Rhonda committed to doing the hard work of developing her personal presence, and it paid off. The Board approved her proposal. When I checked back a few months later to find out how it was going, she said, "Be careful what you ask for! I have never been busier, and I have never been more satisfied with my career."

Be careful of your thoughts,
they become words.

Be careful of your words,
they become actions.

Be careful of your actions,
they become habits.

Be careful of your habits,
they become character.

Be careful of your character,
it becomes your destiny.

- Unknown

Coaching Session

Take some time to figure out your backstory. In what ways is it keeping you from moving forward and taking risks? What emotional potholes do you need to pave over this year?

Start by focusing on a challenge, a wish, a goal, or a need you have in your life right now. Write it down here:

Now describe your doubts, fears or self-limiting beliefs that may be hindering your ability to realize your goal. Be specific and honest.

How does what you just wrote contribute to your emotional backstory? Where do those doubts and fears come from?

Now, answer this question: Is it still true? Y_____ N_____

If your answer is no, go to the final question.

If your answer is yes, what is the strongest self-limiting belief you hold about this story?

Who will you be and what will you gain if you could let go of this belief?

What immediate steps can you take to erase this backstory for good?

The Hat Trick of Personal Presence

For those readers who would rather watch paint dry than sit in a cold ice hockey rink, allow me a bit of latitude with the sports reference. In the game of ice hockey, a hat trick is a pretty cool thing and a beloved tradition. When a player scores three times in one game, fans don't just jump up and cheer, they also throw their hats onto the ice. Most players go through their entire career without scoring a hat trick. Luckily, the chances of scoring a personal presence hat trick are much more attainable. Before we delve into the three types of goals to score, we first have to withstand a small amount of nerdy science that has caused 40 years of consternation.

Albert Mehrabian is a professor at UCLA who is best known for his research on verbal and non-verbal communication. Back in 1968, he conducted research on various types of communication and their impact on the listener.[7] Mehrabian found the most effective communicators align their words, tone of voice, and body language for maximum effect. His key finding is that our body language (the non-verbal communication) is more important than the words or the voice. The resulting equation is the average listener gleans 55% from the speaker's body language, 38% from the speaker's tone of voice, and 7% from the actual words spoken. Soon after the article was published, the equation became known as the 55/38/7 Rule, or the Mehrabian Formula.

The findings were met with considerable pushback from other communication experts who claimed the results were wrong and would mislead the public into thinking word choice was as inconsequential as to be merely an afterthought. In his follow-up book entitled *Silent Messages*, Mehrabian attempted to clarify that his findings were misinterpreted. In point of fact, his research dealt specifically with the expression of emotions (feelings and attitudes). Therefore, the equation had no bearing on any other type of communication such as giving directions, say, or explaining why you were late, or if you wanted fries with that.

Observing the fallout from his findings over the years and the degree to which both sides are fervent in their positions, I am reminded of a WWF Smackdown. Since this is our sports analogy section, I thought it might be fun to sum up the original research (and why you should care) into an imaginary cage fight. Here's what the play-by-play announcer might say:

> First up: Words vs. Tone of Voice. Three grueling rounds to see which one matters more. Round one has the two adversaries saying certain words in a positive way like honey, thanks, and great; round two they must say words like maybe, really, and so in a neutral way; and the toughest round is the negative words like don't, brute, and scram. Round for round they went at each other with gusto, but the clear winner is...Tone of Voice! Final score: Voice 38 – Words 7. But can Voice keep the momentum going as it attempts to defeat the biggest, baddest example of body language in Mehrabian's research? Stay Tuned!

> We're back! Onto the second match-up of the night: this is for the whole enchilada. The Voice is feeling confident after its decisive victory over Words, but does it have what it takes to defeat Facial Expressions? Three more rounds and we have a winner. Tone of Voice put on a great show, but Facial Expressions wins by a mile! Final score: Facial Expressions 55 – Voice 38.

The key takeaway is a person can say the word "scram" and still be seen as likeable because she says it with a smile. "Go on now, scram, before I invite you in and regret it in the morning!" Conversely, a person can utter a normally positive word like "great" and it can sound negative based solely on the tone of voice. "A flat tire...that's just great!" Over the years, the "Mehrabian Formula" has morphed into a more colorful description: "the words, the music and the dance." This is so much better, and thus demonstrating words really do matter.

Now let's look at where the hat trick comes in. Anyone wanting to enhance their personal presence can start by reflecting on how they communicate across these three channels. How effectively they use words, how interesting their voice can be, and how well they dance. Let's look at each of them separately.

The Words

We've already covered the downside of mitigated speech and the fact that we make decisions about word choices both consciously and unconsciously. Another helpful reminder is to be wary of using loaded language, which is the silent killer of open dialogue. Two examples of loaded language are "always" and "never." The bottom line on word choice is people with a strong personal presence are never vague. Some situations call for poetry and others call for simple and straightforward prose. Developing personal presence means we learn to make better decisions about what each situation calls for, and as a result, we spend more time drawing our listener in, instead of sending them far, far away.

The Music

The fastest way to lose the attention of your listener is to speak in a monotone voice. Flat, lifeless voices suck the oxygen (and the fun) right out of the room. If you are a monotone speaker, you will benefit greatly by practicing vocal variety, which is a core skill for any engaging speaker. The only thing more unpleasant is the sound of the vuvuzelas heard non-stop at South African soccer games. I'm still recovering from the World Cup games in 2010, which is why I brought it up as a comparison. Don't let your vocal delivery detract from your otherwise engaging personality.

A monotone voice is bad enough, but it's not the only way to diminish your personal presence. There is another bad habit that goes by the name of Valley Girl Syndrome (VGS). Pay close attention if you are under the age of 35 because odds are you grew up speaking this way. People who suffer from VGS have a tendency to make every phrase and sentence sound like a question.

Another term for VGS is up-talking, which I use in a couple of other instances in future chapters. The only way to eliminate it is to hear it in your own voice. To do that, you need a friend or trusted colleague to make a face or slap the table every time they hear you up-talk. Once you are aware of when and where you throw in a verbal question mark, then you are ready to work on eliminating the bad habit altogether. Remember, if it took you 12 years to perfect your upward inflection, it's going to take more than 12 minutes to get rid of it. Here are a few tips to help you reach your goal.

Sentence structure. Try to avoid speaking in short phrases that can lull you into up-talking: One time? At band camp? My tuba? It, like, fell in the water? And I had to jump in to get it. Those five clauses can be restructured so they come out in a more professional, inviting, and declarative manner. One re-write might be: While I was a band camp last summer my tuba fell in the water and the next thing I knew I was jumping off the dock to get it.

Record yourself. You don't even need one of those old school tape recorders with the teeny tiny cassettes. Just use the recording app on your smart phone. If you can't find it, you can easily download the free iTalk recording app from griffintechnology.com. Press record and start speaking on a very familiar topic, like what you had for breakfast or your biggest pet peeve in life. Then play it back and listen for the inverted ski slope. Repeat this process until there are only well-placed inflections.

Read aloud. Seriously, this is one of the best tips. I guarantee you will not misplace anything when you read aloud, unless the sentence calls for it. Try it. Go to the appendix to see poet Taylor Mali's *Speak With Conviction* text. It's great.

Note: all three of these techniques also help to eliminate a monotone voice, especially reading aloud. To get even more benefit from the exercise, imagine you are reading to a group of 4-yr-olds.

The Dance

You've probably heard the old saying "it takes more muscles to frown than it does to smile" so by golly, turn that frown upside down! I have yet to find definitive scientific research that proves the veracity of this claim, but it sure sounds good. What we *do* know is humans have roughly 43 muscles in the face and if someone smiles using only the muscles of the cheeks and mouth, then they are being insincere. Genuine smiles require the muscles of the eyes to contract as well, and when you combine a true smile with authentic eye contact, you have two core elements of "the dance" working in your favor.

You don't need to remember the Mehrabian Formula to convey engaging personal presence. What matters most is all three aspects of communication – the words, the music and the dance – work in harmony with each other. For example, if you wanted to say thank you to someone who really stepped up, you would look them in the eye, offer a genuine smile of appreciation, probably lean in a little closer to them, maybe even put a hand on their arm and express how grateful you are. Your voice would be in concert with your verbal and non-verbal expressions. If you were truly touched you might speak a little softer and possibly at a lower or higher pitch than your "fill it up with unleaded" voice. If you were excited by what the other person did for you – like offer you two tickets to a Broadway show – your voice would be a lot louder and higher in pitch.

As we end this chapter with a final coaching session, it is helpful to identify one particular area of your life that sparks energy and a sense of hope. Then, try to let that feeling spill over into other aspects of your life.

"Knowing is not enough,
we must apply.
Being willing is not enough,
we must do."

- Leonardo Da Vinci

Coaching Session

The following questions are designed to give you greater insight into the messages you send through your personal presence. It is helpful to evaluate yourself in two ways – the degree to which you *express* yourself and convey authenticity, and the degree to which you are *receptive* to the needs and emotions of others.

Expressive: How composed are you in unfamiliar situations?

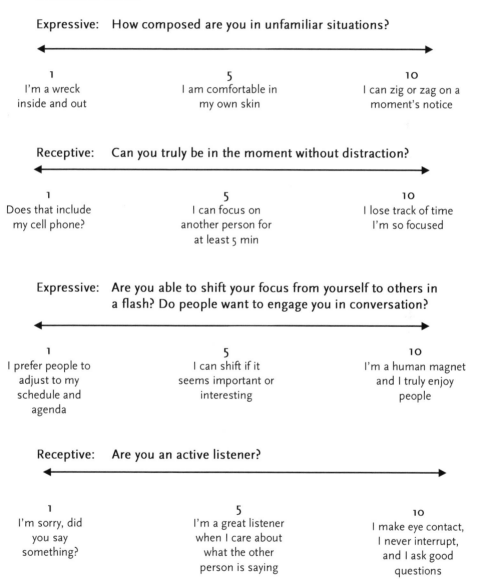

1	5	10
I'm a wreck inside and out	I am comfortable in my own skin	I can zig or zag on a moment's notice

Receptive: Can you truly be in the moment without distraction?

1	5	10
Does that include my cell phone?	I can focus on another person for at least 5 min	I lose track of time I'm so focused

Expressive: Are you able to shift your focus from yourself to others in a flash? Do people want to engage you in conversation?

1	5	10
I prefer people to adjust to my schedule and agenda	I can shift if it seems important or interesting	I'm a human magnet and I truly enjoy people

Receptive: Are you an active listener?

1	5	10
I'm sorry, did you say something?	I'm a great listener when I care about what the other person is saying	I make eye contact, I never interrupt, and I ask good questions

1

chapter summary | cultivating personal presence

If this chapter were...	it would be...
a song	*Express Yourself* by Madonna
a movie	Working Girl
summed up in a famous quote	*"A bird doesn't sing because it has an answer, It sings because it has a song."* - Maya Angelou
rolled up into one word	Energy
condensed into one piece of advice	Never leave your mind and your heart at home. Do more than show up; engage.

chapter 2: landing your dream job

*"I came off of that stage and I knew that I was home. In all my years
of being discontent, feeling like something's not quite right,
feeling like I was in the wrong place, in the wrong job,
I knew this was it. I felt like I could be myself."*

– Oprah Winfrey

You may have heard the statistic that the average person will change careers at least seven times in their lifetime. Or was it seven jobs in a lifetime? This factoid has bounced around for so long without ever being validated by supporting research that it is now meaningless. The truth is, no one really knows for sure how many times the average person changes careers because it is difficult to pin down exactly what constitutes a career change. In a study conducted in 2008, researchers found the average person holds a job for 4.1 years, which calculates to approximately ten jobs in a lifetime.[8]

Wouldn't it be great if one of those jobs felt like your dream job? The kind of work that makes you jump out of bed in the morning full of anticipation for another great day at work? Landing that kind of job can come down to one simple task: selling yourself. To do that, it helps to have a healthy dose of self-worth, a positive outlook, and the conviction that you are the right person for the job. Not just one of the best candidates, but the right candidate. Just wanting the job is not enough, and in certain circumstances, that type of wishful thinking can come across as tentative or even desperate. The best mindset is the enthusiastic, can-do type that sends a "look no further" message to your interviewer.

This chapter is designed to help you develop the right mindset to land your dream job. It is not about where to find job openings or what career is right for you. Instead, my focus is on helping you develop the right attitude, which will come in particularly handy if you find yourself competing with an alpha male, who will *bring it*. I will also offer some best practices and useful tips to help you stand out from the crowd. Candidates for job interviews get one chance to make a great impression and that chance starts the moment you walk in the door.

Do You Know Your Strengths?

Concepts like "core competency" often devolve into buzzwords despite their legitimacy. This is one I'd like to pull back from the brink. Like all over-used jargon, the term core competency started out with good intentions. In its first iteration back in 1990, it was used to define an organization's ability to gain an edge over its competitors by integrating the skills, know-how and expertise that contributed significantly to their success.

Today, core competency is synonymous with an individual's key capabilities. Each of us develops our own core competency over time by focusing and being diligent, by staying motivated and soliciting feedback, and by making a commitment to improve. Another important aspect is that one's core competency should improve with continued use. The more time you spend doing something, the more skilled you become.

Should you spend time defining your core competency? The answer depends on whether or not you will ever want to or need to stand out from the crowd, and if you want to feel more confident in unfamiliar situations.

Before we delve into the process of identifying your core competency, let's start with an insider's look into the search process most organizations use to find the perfect candidate. Across all industries and job titles, recruiters and search committees utilize the following criteria to screen applicants:

Level 1: Baseline. These skills and attributes help you get your foot in the door. Recruiters expect to find these skills on every resume. One example might be that you are reliable or a hard worker, or you are proficient in Microsoft Word.

Level 2: Distinctive. People with distinctive capabilities get their resume put in the "A" pile instead of the recycle bin. These qualifiers help you get noticed. An example of this level might be chairing your company's first strategic planning committee. Or perhaps you have a demonstrated ability to manage large, high-profile projects.

Level 3: Competitive Advantage. This level is considered rarified air because these competencies are hard to come by; they can take years to develop, but once acquired, they play a critical role in your success. Examples of competitive advantage often involve revenue generation, cost savings, or the ability to supervise others. They can also be a result of specialized training such as certified project management professional or advanced database specialist. There are other ways to attain level three competencies that do not involve further education or having a management-level job.

For example, one of my clients, let's call her Sydney, took the initiative to create a community service event that raised over ten thousand dollars for a high-need charity. That wasn't what set her apart from other go-getters. The differentiator was she invited the local press to cover the event and they showed up. She was then able to set up an interview for her CEO to speak on local TV, and talk about his company in a positive light. She was given a big bonus for all her hard work, and several months later was offered a promotion.

When I heard the news I extended my sincere congratulations and then said the next thing that popped into my head, which was, "You made this all look so easy. None of my other clients are going to believe this story. Get your boss on TV to promote the company and poof! – a bonus and a promotion. Would you let me talk to your boss to get his perspective?" And she said, in complete confidence, "Of course!"

A few days later I was able to reach the CEO and I asked him to give me his perspective on Sydney's amazing year. He said he was very impressed with her ability to pull off the fundraiser without missing a step in her regular job. He went on to say that from his perspective, she did something very important for all the employees – she helped them remember they were on the same team. "After the event, everyone was re-energized and happy to be at work. You can't put a price on that."

I then asked him to describe Sydney in one sentence. He said, "She's the most productive person on my staff, she is always positive, and she can say 'no' without ruffling any feathers. I don't know how she does it."

Do you think your boss could describe your capabilities in similarly impressive terms? If your answer is yes, then go for it – find a time to ask for that feedback. If the answer is no, then the coaching sessions in this book will help you turn no into a yes.

Oh, and one more thing. Think of core competency as a muscle – you lose it if you don't use it.

"When you're in a bad mood,
you're better at "what's wrong here?"
When you're in a good mood, you're better at
"what's right here?"

- Martin Seligman, Flourish

Coaching Session

This is one of several exercises designed to help you excavate your personal strengths and unique qualities so you gain confidence to step up and stand out from the crowd. This particular exercise is helpful to gain clarity on your personal efficacy. How do you show up in the world and what do you have to offer the employer of your dream job?

First, make a list of your core capabilities. Think of these skills and attributes as falling into two categories: the "know-what" and "know-how." They are skills, talents and specialized knowledge you are proud of, that have helped you navigate your way through various challenges, and that boost your confidence. Don't worry so much about which capability fits into which box, but rather getting them all down on paper.

Know-What Capabilities	Know-How Capabilities
Knowledge, aptitude, expertise, etc.	Skills, actions, attitudes, beliefs, etc.
Ex: formal learning, academic background, diplomas, certificates, industry expertise.	Ex: supporting customers, improving the shipping process, managing a project, software specialist.

Now try to write a sentence that weaves all of these capabilities together into a core competency. For example, when I asked one of my career coaching clients (a spitfire of a woman who never minced words) to summarize her capabilities into one sentence she said, "I get shit done!" Perhaps you want to go into more detail than that, but if a bumper sticker gets you jazzed up then that's great, too. Write it down and then say it out loud just to hear how it sounds.

Don't Sit on Your Assets

There is a new home going up right outside my window. All day long I hear the clamor of construction – pneumatic hammers, back-up beeps and rock blasting equipment. Some days I'm happy to start the dishwasher just to balance out the cacophony of noises. The other day, right around dusk, I sensed something was different. I realized that the neighborhood was quiet. Every nerve-wracking power tool was turned off.

I looked out and saw the silhouettes of the construction crew against the greying sky. They moved around like dancers, graceful and fluid. They strode across the roof beam as if they were on solid ground. I started to get a zen-like feeling as I watched them conduct their final tasks for the day, appearing to have no concern for the fading light, almost as if they didn't need it. And then it dawned on me: I was watching "unconscious competence" in action (see figure below).

Unconscious competence is the final phase of Noel Birch's Four Stages of Competence.[9] People who are unconsciously competent are so skilled in a particular task that they no longer have to think about it. It's a worthy aim for any practitioner, but no one can achieve that level without hard work, self-directed learning, feedback, and a commitment to improve.

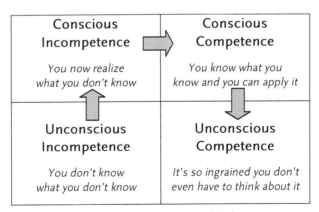

Four Stages of Competence by Noel Burch

In my coaching practice, I often find that clients have some core gift or skill that they have overlooked when they feel pressure to develop another skill. I try to point them out so that these skills can be called upon when it's time to make a positive impression or convince someone they are the right person for the job. Some people have a way with words. Others have a great sense of humor. One recent client had expert knowledge in a highly-regarded sales technique, but she was so concerned about having no experience supervising others that she under-sold herself.

Unconscious competence is the final stage of a four-stage process, and while a worthwhile goal for all the perks that come along with it, should never be taken for granted. Even the most gifted practitioner must refresh and renew their skills. Otherwise, unconscious competence turns into complacency.

One of the best books of 2012 is Martin Seligman's *Flourish* in which he uncovers the latest research on motivation, optimism and character. My favorite section of the book focuses on emotional fitness – specifically, our ability to tap into positive emotions and resist catastrophic thoughts.[10] My reaction to this concept was "Where do I sign up?!" Capitalizing on positive emotions is possible when we become more aware of our triggers. That is, the situations that elicit negative thoughts and why; and the situations that elicit positive thoughts. Then it's a matter of using our self-control, which is one of Seligman's core elements of positive character, and of having "grit" – the personality characteristic of "extreme persistence."

He also offers the best definition of a signature strength I've ever come across. Here it is:

> *"A 'signature strength' is invigorating rather than exhausting.*
> *It is so much a part of your positive self that if someone told you*
> *to tone it down or stop using it, you would say 'Try to stop me.'"*

Is it just me or does this definition improve your outlook on life? Does it make you feel energized and ready to take an inventory of your double Ss? Well then, let's get started.

Coaching Session

Borrowing from Seligman's book, take a moment to answer the following questions:

Think back on a time when you felt one of the positive emotions: pride, gratitude, pleasure, satisfaction, interest, hope. Jot down a few details about the situation/memory you chose.

Now, in what ways could this situation/feeling be applied more consistently to optimize your life?

Next, write down at least two of your "signature strengths" using the definition on the previous page. You know it's a signature strength if you feel proud or happy to say it out loud. Remember, no mitigated speech! After you have finished writing, do say it out loud (or even better, speak it to someone you respect and ask for feedback).

How can these signature strengths help you in a job interview?

What do you most want to be known for when the interview process is over and the employer is deciding on which candidate to hire?

How to Answer Questions with Aplomb

Maybe you are one of those people who relishes a challenge and are always excited about a job interview. Good for you. Feel free to skate right past this chapter. Otherwise, let's focus on one of the most important aspects of landing your dream job: answering interview questions. I know I would be preaching to the choir if I advised you to do your research on your target company before showing up for the interview. It would be the equivalent of saying, "Excuse me, your phone is ringing," just as you press the answer button. Once you have all the essential information about who you are meeting with and what the organization is all about, you can prepare your responses to potential questions. Here are some helpful tips:

Find your focus. The first way to hit the mark with your answers is to identify the type of question being asked. Is it informational (how long were you with the circus?), speculative (what if you could never tame another tiger–would you still be happy?), personality style (what type of work environment suits you best?), work history (what did you do before the circus act?), or is the interviewer trying to gauge how well you think on your feet (if you could have dinner with one famous person, living or dead, who would it be?). Once you have your focus, you will have a much better chance of staying in control, and have an easier job of aligning your answer with what the interviewer is looking for.

Answer the question that was asked <u>and then stop talking</u>. Too often, in our undying need to impress the interviewer, we answer three additional unasked questions. This is a recipe for disaster. Not only could you find yourself in a verbal *cul de sac*, but you end up talking too long and then petering out in an unpolished manner.

Don't stumble on the softball questions. Nervous applicants often view every question like it's Mt. Everest; that it will take everything they have to thoroughly answer the question. In fact, several questions should feel like a walk in the park because they are the opposite of "gotcha" questions. Stay relaxed and in the moment so that when you hear a question like "How long were you at Dunder Mifflin?" your answer can be one complete sentence.

If you don't know the answer, don't panic. Never fabricate an answer or evade the question. If it's a matter of not understanding what was asked, try to re-phrase it and ask for verification. That buys you all kinds of time to create a plan of action. If it's a matter of not knowing how to answer the question, for example, those think-on-your-feet questions like "If you were an amusement park ride, which one would you be?", then do what the pros do and say "I'm not familiar enough with amusement parks to choose the one that would fit me best, but what I *can* tell you is..." This transition can get you out of a jam better than most other options as long as you have a good ending to it. Think of it as pivoting. You are simply leading the interviewer to a more promising conversational thread that re-focuses them on the reason why they should hire you.

Remember to use STAR to structure your answers. Most job interviews are heavily focused on questions that start with "Tell me about a time when..." The purpose is to get you to talk about your skills, knowledge, personality style or work experience in a way that will help the interviewer winnow down the applicant pool. These questions are great because they give you an opportunity to brag in a very unboastful way about your unique attributes and successes. The best way to answer these questions is by describing the **situation**/example, then specify the particular **task**/challenge you were asked to take on, then share the **actions** you took to complete the task (resolve the issue), and the **result**(s) you were able to achieve. You can't go wrong.

Don't wear out your welcome. Try to keep every answer as succinct as possible. The timing we should all shoot for is under one minute for each answer. Of course, this is a general guideline. Some can be longer, and many more could be shorter. The point is to not over-explain. Interviewers like nothing more than to talk about their organization and you will be better off for having saved time for them to do just that.

Take full advantage when the ball is passed to you. As soon as you hear the interviewer ask, "Do you have any questions for me?" take it as your cue to shine. Demonstrate your knowledge of the company by asking questions that give them an opportunity to share some recent successes and current challenges they might be facing.

It's also helpful to ask a couple of questions that telegraph how you could contribute to their success. The only way to tarnish your reputation is to ask about money, vacation, benefits, and other human resource-related matters. All other questions could lead to a conversation about you as the person in the job.

I remember serving on a search committee that decided to bring seven candidates onsite for 1-hour interviews. The first four interviews went smoothly, and we were right on schedule. The fifth interview, however, went 25 minutes over schedule simply because the candidate kept on talking and talking until the committee chair stood up and abruptly said, "Thanks, Ron, I think we have enough information!" When the candidate left the room, the chairperson said, "I'm sorry, but I just had to pull the band aid off in one motion!"

Not only was that particular candidate cut from the pool of finalists, but his interview lived on in infamy. Every time someone talked too long in a staff meeting, another colleague would say, "OK 'Ron,' we need to move on!"

"A capability is only as good as its execution."

- Kouzes and Posner, *Credibility*

Coaching Session

The more you practice answering potential interview questions the better you become at staying focused on your key message and avoiding the long-winded response. Practice answering the following questions in a way that highlights your skills, attributes and personality traits. It is best done with a friend or colleague so that you can give each other feedback on your answers.

1. Tell me about yourself.
    Underlying purpose: what makes you unique?

2. Why do you want to work here/go to school here?
    Underlying purpose: what is special about our organization/school?

3. What do you see yourself doing ten years from now?
    Underlying purpose: how do you define success?

4. What is your greatest weakness?
    Underlying purpose: are you a realistic and honest person?

5. Describe a time when you were an effective team player.
    Underlying purpose: do you get along well with others?

6. Tell me about a time when you felt under pressure due to a strict deadline. How did you handle it and what was the result?
    Underlying purpose: can you handle stress/are you self-directed?

7. Describe a recent accomplishment at work.
    Underlying purpose: will you be successful here?

And the assortment of oddball questions that could be asked:

If you were a car, would kind would you be?
What is your favorite movie and why?
What was the last business book you read?
If you were a superhero, what special power would you have?

The Secret to Connecting With Others

I stumbled upon a Charlie Rose interview with TED* curator, Chris Anderson, and it was one of those moments that makes you think more seriously about the power of intention. The timing was perfect. I was getting ready for an important presentation and was thinking about how to approach a very smart, very busy audience. And there was my answer: stop trying to craft a rigorous argument, and instead, fire up their "mirror neurons."

Here is an excerpt from the interview:

Rose: What do the best [speakers] have?

Anderson: They have figured out a way to connect with other people and make them want to care. They have clarity – they don't get lost in jargon. There's a certain empathy that [the best speakers] have...they look listeners in the eye and then share their passion. Something very magical is happening at that point.

Rose: It *is* a magical thing – to see somebody walk into a room and be able to have the audience almost breathing in rhythm.

Anderson: We now know that when one human being exhibits an emotion, the people watching that person have the same mirror neurons firing in their brains. They actually *are* that person for a moment.

The best way to move yourself to the top of the finalist list is to genuinely relate to your interviewer. After all, the entire search process is based on one factor: fit. That is, will you fit in with the culture, and are your particular skills and attributes a fit with the job requirements. One way to prove you are a good fit is to make a genuine connection with everyone you meet during your interview process – and that includes security guards and receptionists.

In a healthy organizational culture, everyone's opinion matters. In one very unfortunate case, the top candidate was not offered her dream job because she ignored the shuttle driver who had driven her to various locations throughout the day. After he dropped her off at the airport, he went straight to the CEO's office and explained how rude she was. The CEO called her that night and said, "No thanks."

*TED: Riveting talks by remarkable people, free to the world – www.ted.com

Mirror neurons explain why humans are capable of great empathy. And they are just sitting there, like little packs of sugar, just waiting to be put to good use. Instead of focusing so hard on avoiding a verbal gaffe, put that energy toward increasing your likeability.

How to Write a Compelling Biographical Sketch (and how to talk about yourself on the spot)

Recruiters can now obtain a lot of information about you by searching the internet. It is important to type your own name in the browser window before starting a job search to be sure there is nothing out there in "the cloud" that would paint a negative picture. I usually save this advice for people who are young enough to have always known a computer disk drive was not a cup holder, but it's fast becoming an important lesson for people of all ages.

One of the more important pieces of information you would want recruiters to find is a biographical sketch – any blurb that sums up who you are and what you offer. If you don't have a website then the next best place is your LinkedIn profile. If you have one already, when was the last time you updated it? If you don't have one yet, then that's the place to start. Be specific and make it compelling.

Every professional should have an interesting, well-written and easily accessible professional biography. The "bio" serves two purposes. First, you are always ready to respond when someone calls and asks for one – whether it's because you are delivering a presentation at a conference or because you are volunteering to organize the United Way Campaign. Second, once it is written out and you are satisfied with how you come across on paper, you can use the content to form your "elevator speech" for interviews, networking events, speed dating, you name it.

Here are a few guidelines to help you write or revise your profile.

1. **It's not a laundry list**; it's a snapshot of what makes you unique and worthy of an interview. Focus more on expertise and capabilities; dim the lights on accolades and awards. Although, if you were voted *Esquire's* Sexiest/Funniest/Happiest Woman of the Year, then by all means include it!

2. **Be specific** about why someone would want to hire you or learn from you. What's your key message? What expectations do you want them to have of you before you step foot on site for an interview? What do you know, what can you offer, how can you solve their problems?

3. **Make it sizzle**, just a little. Think in word pictures. For example, one of my clients is a freelance tax accountant who has to compete with do-it-yourself options such as *TurboTax*. We worked on his elevator speech to make it more vivid and he now tells people that he saves them from tax software hell. He contacted me to say that it was turning out to be a very effective description because so many people understand how that feels and that they never want to feel that stress again.

4. **Close with a personal tidbit.** After you share any relevant academic background, think about a particular hobby, interest, or passion that might add a little flavor to balance out the necessary factual information. People are interested in other people, not chronology.

"The thing women have yet to learn
is nobody *gives* you power.
You just take it."

- Roseanne Barr

Coaching Session

Do you have an attention-getting narrative? Have it handy while you do this exercise. If you don't have one, then this activity is definitely worth your time. Start by filling in the boxes below:

Current and past work history	Education and training, awards	Unique personality traits	Expertise, knowledge, skills	Hobbies, interests, etc.

Once you have enough content in each box, try to write out a paragraph that incorporates all the things you believe are worth sharing – the things that will make your reader/listener think. "I want to meet this person" or "I want to listen to this person."

_____

_____

_____

_____

_____

_____

_____

_____

_____

_____

Love it or Hate it, It's All About the Networking

There seem to be two kinds of people in this world – those who love to network and those who would rather poke themselves in the eye with a sharp stick than enter a roomful of strangers. Whichever side you come down on, it's important to know that over 60% of jobs are found through networking. With those kinds of numbers, it would be a mistake to limit your face-to-face networking activities. Online networking is necessary in the 21st century, but it is insufficient.

I remember working with a group of college seniors who were getting ready to attend their first national conference. The primary purpose was to find a job, but they were also going to learn more about their industry and to be better prepared to enter their field of choice. I kept saying to them, "Walk right up to the senior leader and introduce yourself. Don't hesitate because you will regret it when you get back home." The majority of them were squirming in their seats. Hands shot up to ask some version of the same question, "But what do I say?!" "I'll sound stupid or they'll think I'm just using them to get a job."

We discussed all the ways they could engage a hiring authority in a conversation. They practiced their elevator pitches until they were succinct and compelling, and with a final "seize the day!" cheer from me, off they went. Sure enough, when they came back, I received several emails with exciting updates, but one student in particular showed up at my office to share her networking success story. I noticed she was smiling from ear to ear so I knew it would be pretty special. Turns out on the second day of the conference she found herself standing in a slow-moving line at a luncheon buffet. As she waited for the gentlemen in front of her to move forward, she noticed his name tag and realized she was standing next to the #1 person on her networking wish list: the CEO of the company she most wanted to work for.

Remembering my advice, she took a deep breath and dove into the deep end. By the time they had gotten through the buffet line, he had invited her to dine with him so they could continue talking. By the end of the conference she had a job interview lined up. And that is what networking can do. That is why networking is so important.

What other ways could you meet a key decision-maker? By assuming every stranger is no more than six degrees separated from the person you are trying to meet. Another term for this is the 30-foot rule. Anyone within 30 feet of you could be a direct or indirect connection to your dream job. Networking cuts through all the red tape of online resume submissions and key word searches and over-worked screening committees. It can level the playing field, and it can help you stand out from the crowd.

The Fab Four of Networking

1. Be a magnet, not a windsock. Rather than sending out the "please hire me" vibe, shift your focus to drawing people toward you with welcoming eye contact, a smile and a verbal greeting, and then engage him or her in a dynamic conversation. A good rule of thumb is to listen 70% of the time and talk 30%.

2. Know your pitch. Your elevator speech is your ticket to a deeper, more productive conversation. Your delivery should take no longer than 30 seconds and should be positive and enticing. What makes you interesting? What are you passionate about? Practice often.

3. Come prepared. First, be smart and pick your events carefully. More is not better. Find out who'll be in attendance, and then research the organization or executive. Be ready with one or two questions and perhaps a positive comment about what you find most interesting about their organization. In addition to business cards, a name tag, and appropriate attire, the right attitude is a must. Would you show up at the grocery store without your wallet? In addition to questions about the organization, it is also helpful to have a few conversation starters ready to go. Checking online news sources before you head out is a great way to feel more prepared to make small talk.

4. Manage the clock. It's not about how many people you meet; it's about making meaningful connections and leaving a lasting impression. When people think you are barreling through the event trying to beat the networking record, you leave them with a sour aftertaste. That said, do try to limit each conversation to approximately seven minutes. That gives you enough time to interact without getting stuck. If you do get stuck in a conversation, excuse yourself to refresh your beverage and then do exactly that.

2

chapter summary | landing your dream job

If this chapter were...	it would be...
a song	*Girl on Fire* by Alicia Keys
a movie	The Pursuit of Happiness
summed up in a famous quote	*"Communication – the human connection – is the key to personal and career success."* - Paul Meyer
rolled up into one word	Initiative
condensed into one piece of advice	Rather than trying to be perfect in a job interview, focus more on letting your true personality shine through.

chapter 3: speaking in public

"Have you ever had an itch and not scratched it?
The scratching gives immediate relief.
What if that itch was insecurity or self-hatred?
Then the only way to heal is to find ways to work with the itch –
a willingness to do something for yourself – to connect with
your own strength, your own wisdom, your own confidence."

- Pema Chodron

Let me ask you a question. What can increase your self-confidence, make you feel incredibly powerful, offer an enormous degree of satisfaction, and advance your career all at the same time? No, not hot yoga. No, not Red Bull. The answer is public speaking.

Sounds wonderful doesn't it? How many skill sets can offer as much return on investment? Yet many people shy away from speaking opportunities no matter how small. The resistance often comes from the "what if" syndrome: What if I forget what I'm going to say? What if I say something really stupid? What if the audience doesn't like me? The what-ifs then diminish our tolerance for risk-taking and the result is we lose out on the rewards that could come with stepping onto center stage.

This chapter focuses on the tips and techniques that will enable you to stand up and speak in public with skill, style and increased confidence.

The #1 Reason Why You Fear Public Speaking

I once worked with two change management experts who spent several years on the speaking circuit together. They were always more impressive when they presented as a team. We'll call them Ted and Deborah. Each time an upcoming presentation loomed on the calendar, Deborah would ask Ted to carve out a few hours to prepare. And every time, Ted said he was really busy, and not to worry, because they'd be great.

When I finally inquired about this dynamic, Ted said he preferred to be extemporaneous and in the moment. And to his credit, he is adept at impromptu speaking – one of the best I've ever seen. Deborah said that unless she thoroughly prepared, she was a complete wreck and her fear would invariably win out. For the entire presentation her anxiety would be in the red zone. She would then go home vowing never to speak in public again. She is otherwise an intelligent, articulate and talented person.

These two individuals fall on opposite ends of my public speaking continuum. Before we continue, try plotting yourself on the graph.

I'd rather dodge traffic than speak in public	With alcohol or beta blockers I'm pretty good	I won't volunteer, but I got skills	I'm great if it's a topic I know really well	I'm a fearless zen ninja warrior

If you placed yourself anywhere on the left side of the range, the good news is your anxiety has nothing to do with your abilities or your worthiness. The knee-knocker symptoms stem from the part of the brain known as the amygdala, which is in charge of our emotional reactions. When we are overwhelmed, the amygdala decides to put up a Jersey Barrier to our rational brain. In extreme cases, we experience what Daniel Goleman calls an amygdala hijack.[11] A powerful example of this concept is the outburst by Serena Williams at the 2009 U.S. Open tennis championship at which she "screamed her way out of the tournament" arguing with the line judge about a foot fault.[12]

Most of us will never experience an amygdala hijack on such a public stage, but we are equally capable of thwarting our chances of delivering a great presentation, a memorable toast, or a killer job interview. Brain researchers at Stanford University found that the amygdala is not well connected to the region of the brain responsible for determining the importance of stimuli. "This could mean that people have a harder time discerning truly worrisome situations from mild annoyances. People who suffer from general anxiety disorder feel overwhelmed by emotion and don't believe they can feel sad or upset without coming completely undone. So, in an attempt to avoid facing their unpleasant feelings, they distract themselves by fretting."[13] This is an apt description of Deborah who worked herself into a tizzy before every presentation.

Life is too short to let a self-defeating mindset dictate our success. Amygdala shmygdala. Let's do this right. Women should know how to change a tire, which fork to use, and how to banish the jimjams.

Jimjams, n., the jitters. - Merriam Webster Dictionary

The Only Way to Boost Your Confidence *Before* a Presentation

The other day I was walking past a couple of guys having lunch, and I heard one of them say, "My big presentation is tomorrow and I've had no time to practice." At this I slowed my pace so I could officially eavesdrop on their conversation. He continued, "Well, that's not exactly true. I've been rehearsing it in my head." To which the other guy said, "Then you'll be fine." Now picture me forcing one foot in front of the other so I wouldn't lean over the booth and yell "Are you crazy?! Think about your audience and their expectations. Get back to the office and practice!"

No, he will not be fine. And, yes, I might have raised my voice if I had inserted myself into their conversation. The presentation will be filled with ums and ahs, and will meander all over hell's half-acre, all to the beat of the tentative drum in his head. If he's lucky, his PowerPoint slides will save him from a brain freeze, but odds are he'll use all 75 of them as a crutch. Rehearsing "in your head" is not a rehearsal. Unless you actually hear your voice saying the words you wrote by hand or typed on the computer (at a volume of 7 out of 10), you are not rehearsing.

I have to admit I have sinned on occasion, much in the same way a doctor tells her patients to eat better and then has ice cream for lunch. My most recent lapse nearly cost me a steady client. I was asked to give a team-building seminar to a group of middle managers from a company I had worked with in the past. In my head I was thinking "walk-off home run without needing even one practice swing." My handout looked great. My slides were a feast for the human eye. What more did I need to do? Better to use any free time searching the web for adorable puppy videos.

As Julia Roberts' character in *Pretty Woman* says, "Big mistake — huge." Six hours before the seminar I got a call from the client saying I should expect eight additional attendees who would be there to "observe." When I asked who those people might be, the client said, "Various directors and vice presidents who want to get some ideas from you." Suddenly, I wasn't ready. Suddenly, I had no idea what I was planning to say because, in all honesty, I felt I could wing it. Now I needed to revisit my content and practice. My favorite way to do this is to turn on the video recorder, do a practice round, and play it back. Yes, it's painful, but it is so effective.

I'm happy to say the seminar was a success. Not only was I more articulate, but my timing was better and I had ready answers to their questions because I spent the time thinking through what might be asked and what I could offer. The eight observers all stayed for the entire seminar and several approached me afterward to thank me for providing them with some useful tools to help them boost team productivity.

This is a cautionary tale about the role practice plays in feeling confident about standing up in front of an audience. Preparation alone is not enough. Factor in the time to speak out loud to yourself, your pet, or your significant other — it doesn't matter who — and you stand a better chance of feeling competent and confident.

How to Overcome a Crisis of Confidence

So, you've prepared *and* practiced. You feel so sure of your content and your purpose that you're thinking, "Put me in coach, I'm ready!" You can see the whole thing in your mind's eye: the rapt attention of your audience; commanding the physical space like a sensei;

technology working seamlessly, including state-of-the art audio. At the end you receive vigorous applause from the crowd, which is well-deserved because you earned it. You, my friend, are a public speaking rock star.

But then reality kicks in. As you walk into the room it dawns on you that everything is wrong. The tables are too far away. The lighting is way too dark. The projector placement will inhibit your ability to move around. But wait, there's more! The only microphone available is the one wired into the lectern, and worst of all, the event host tells you that because they are running so late, you are to start your presentation...wait for it...during dinner.

This is not a risk manager's doomsday scenario. It happens all the time. Without a Plan B, all sorts of mayhem and foolishness can ensue.[14] If you find yourself in this position, keep one thing in mind: the audience doesn't know you are changing things on the fly. Whatever you do, don't give it away by offering a long-winded explanation or telegraphing your feelings with tense body language, or worst of all, apologizing. Every presenter learns how to adjust to the last-minute curve balls so their performance is in no way diminished by a data projector with a dead bulb. What matters most is that _you_ show up, fully present and ready to engage. The rest is fluff.

Let's examine *how* we manage to impede our own success. Quite simply, through distorted thinking, or, what is known in 12-step programs as "stinkin' thinkin'." Look at the following ways in which we can easily drain ourselves of any positive emotion. Perhaps you'll want to put a checkmark near the ones that feel familiar. You might even feel like you invented one or two of these thought patterns.

Overanalyzing	Catastrophizing
Magnifying	Blaming
Overgeneralization	Polarization
Personalizing	Filtering out the positive
Discrediting	Worthlessness

Being a card-carrying Type A with a unique capacity to summon enormous amounts of energy on a dime, I am very good at convincing myself those curve balls headed toward me are disasters in the making, which then leads to a complete unraveling of all the positive thoughts I had prior to the first sign of trouble.

I remember the time when I was walking to my car, which was parked on the street in the city of Boston, and noticed my front headlights were smashed. My first reaction was fear, which quickly morphed into anger, which then looped back around and came out as helplessness. Luckily I was with my sister Janet who is an auto mechanic. Yup, you read that sentence correctly, my sister the auto mechanic.

When she saw me throw my hands up in exasperation, she looked at me calmly and said "All we need to do is go to the store and get a couple of bulbs." Within a half hour we were on the road as if nothing had happened. I vowed right then to stop over-reacting before I had all the facts; to slow down my thought process and try to analyze the situation in order to make better decisions. I knew myself well enough to realize I would need some help and inspiration.

My search for a calming influence led me to the teachings of Pema Chodron. For those readers who are not familiar with her work, allow me to introduce you. Pema is a former elementary school teacher turned Tibetan Buddhist nun who runs the Gampo Abbey in Nova Scotia. She is smart and thoughtful and caring, and has done the hard work of brutally honest self-discovery and practicing forgiveness – what she calls "loving kindness." My first encounter with her work was through an audiobook I popped into the CD player on a long car ride, honestly not expecting much. The audiobook was called *Getting Unstuck*.[15]

The most eye-opening aspect of her talk focused on why we allow our "critical mind" to take over and send us all manner of negative, self-critical messages. The Tibetan word for this mindset is "shenpa," which means attachment, but as Pema explains, the word attachment absolutely does not get at the true meaning, so the more helpful translation is, "how we get hooked" – when we internalize hurt, anger, remorse, or regret – and then get stuck in that place. Referring back to the quote at the beginning of this chapter, Shenpa is the itch that causes us to overeat, have one more drink, beat ourselves up, or snap at a loved one for no apparent reason. Here's Pema in her own words:

> "Somebody says a mean word to you and then something in you tightens. That's the shenpa. Then it starts to spiral into low self-esteem, or blaming, or anger, or denigrating yourself. This is a mean word that gets you, hooks you. Another word might not affect you, but we're talking about where it touches that sore place – that's a shenpa.
>
> The fundamental root of shenpa is ego-clinging. We experience it as a tightening or self-absorption. It's not the thoughts, it's the emotion. You can feel it happening. And it's never new. It always has a familiar taste and smell. And you are already well into the phase of scratching, turning it against yourself.
>
> These moments teach us to perk up and lean in when we'd rather collapse and back away. They're like messengers that show us, with terrifying clarity, exactly where we're stuck. This very moment is the perfect teacher."

Pema's core message is that only by fully recognizing the ego-clinging and then releasing it can we experience the "cool shade of fearlessness." Otherwise we live our life with a constant buzz of background static. Imagine the worst elevator or on-hold-with-tech-support "musak" you have ever heard and then imagine it always playing in your head. We need to find the off-switch.

How do we get rid of the itch without scratching? Easy to say, and much harder to do. Pema calls it the four Rs:

Recognize, Refrain, Relax, Resolve.

The first step involves acknowledging or seeing the shenpa. Ideally we have caught it before the downward spiral begins, but catching it even after we are hooked is good enough in order to interrupt the momentum.

The next step – and here is where the hard part begins – is to resist the urge to scratch it. That is, refrain from doing the habitual thing that only serves to mask the feelings (for me, it's anything made with white flour). Now comes the third R. Find a quiet place that allows you to relax and settle in so the feelings emerge and then <u>stay there</u>

until you find a whole new perspective on what really happened. Try not to get caught in the play-by-play, but focus on what made you get hooked.

The final step is to make a commitment to not get hooked the next time a similar situation occurs. When I offer this process to my coaching clients and they look at me with a healthy dose of skepticism, I tell them about a time when I managed to work through all four steps and actually released the shenpa. It even feels good to write that sentence. It's the spiritual and mental equivalent of dieting. You can imagine a commercial on tackling shenpa: "I stuck with it through all four Rs and I lost 10 pounds!"

Back to the story. It was during the time when I reported to a bully boss. He was very smart, accomplished, and gregarious, but when it came to supervising people, he could easily become a verbally abusive micromanager. One of his controlling behaviors I found particularly offensive was his tendency to stop any conversation or discussion in its tracks by making the timeout gesture you would see a referee make during a basketball game. It was jarring and it often felt disrespectful. Like a mean version of the Dog Whisperer.

I didn't like what it said about him, but I *really* didn't like what it said about me that I got so hooked. So, I made a commitment to work through the four Rs and figure out why I "went there." I realized the gesture meant I was somehow not performing to his standard and he was dissatisfied with my contribution (or the team's contribution – that's right, I could get hooked for all of us).

I then took the extra step to talk to him about it (in my best "I" voice and using neutral language) and he handled the conversation quite well. He assured me his use of the hand gesture was in no way a judgment on my performance, but more about his responsibility to manage time effectively. He was a stickler for avoiding timewasters, especially anything he felt was a tangent, and that was his way of redirecting the meeting back toward the agenda.

For the remaining time we worked together, our relationship was more productive. We understood each other better and I stopped misinterpreting his non-verbals. A genuine win-win.

Letting go of the uneasiness feels great. To do that, we sometimes need help, and it is my belief that life and career coaching have taken off because of this very reason. Having a supportive, but impartial sounding board to work through the four Rs is extremely helpful.

Public speaking spells shenpa for many people. There's even a medical term for it: glossophobia. Jerry Seinfeld is famous for joking about an old research study on what humans fear most. The first is public speaking, which came in ahead of death. Seinfeld said, "That means we would rather be in the casket than giving the eulogy."

The study he was referring to was conducted in 1973 by R.H. Bruskin Associates and involved over 2500 participants.[16] Each was asked what their greatest fears were and the result was 41% chose speaking in front of a group as their greatest fear out of a list of 14 choices. Critics argue the results are misleading because the choices were not ranked in a particular order, but the overall finding still has relevance. My reaction is this: public speaking is scarier than snakes? But, that's just me.

> "Our deepest fear is not that we are inadequate.
> Our deepest fear is that we are powerful
> beyond measure. It is our light, not our darkness
> that most frightens us. We ask ourselves, 'Who am
> I to be brilliant, gorgeous, talented, fabulous?'
> Actually, who are you not to be?...
> Your playing small does not serve the world."
>
> - Marianne Williamson

Coaching Session

What happens to your mental and emotional state when things go wrong before an important event? Write it down here. Spend a few moments getting in touch with that experience.

Did you write anything that might result in a decrease of positive feelings or genuine anticipation?

Are there things you could do to keep these thoughts and feelings from undermining your success in the future?

Do you know anyone who is consistently and genuinely confident regardless of the situation? What do you observe about him or her?

Is there anything you wrote down that you could start doing or start thinking about yourself?

Manage Your Nerves Like a Hollywood Actor

When comedian Steve Martin was invited to host the academy awards ceremony for the second time he said, "I'm very pleased to be hosting the Oscars again because fear and nausea always make me lose weight." If you have experienced your own version of performance jitters then you are in good company. Many famous performers have battled stage fright, which is proof it doesn't have to hamstring your success. Barbara Streisand and Carly Simon are two examples of successful performers who can be overwhelmed by stage fright before a show. While they may never completely rid themselves of it, they have each found a way to give great performances in spite of their anxiety.

Perhaps the best example of making lemonade out of nervous lemons is comedian Steven Wright who is best known for his droll and deadpan delivery style. As the story goes, he was so nervous during his debut standup act that the audience thought he was in character. They loved it, which gave him all the help he needed to launch his career.

One of my MBA students was so crippled by stage fright that none of my advice seemed to help. I began looking for other ideas that might do the trick. Knowing it is our thoughts that trigger the physical response and not the other way around, I wanted to find a technique that would redirect those negative thoughts before they became a menace. I turned to the acting profession for help.

In my search I came upon the following poem[17] that is attributed to Elia Kazan, the famous actor and director who founded the Actors Studio. I advised my student to recite it a few moments before she stood up to speak, then take a few slow, deep breaths, remember why she was standing there – because she had useful knowledge to share – assume a high-power pose, smile at her audience, and begin to speak.

If you suffer from performance anxiety, you may want to keep this poem nearby. Hey, if it works for Hollywood, it can work for the rest of us. Here it is:

The Actor's Vow

I will take my rightful place on stage
and I will be myself.
I am not a cosmic orphan.
I have no reason to be timid.
I will respond as I feel,
awkwardly, vulgarly,
but respond.

I will have my throat open,
I will have my heart open,
I will be vulnerable.
I may have anything or everything
the world has to offer, but the thing
I need most, and want most,
is to be myself.

I will admit rejection, admit pain,
admit frustration, admit even pettiness,
admit shame, admit outrage,
admit anything and everything
that happens to me.

The best and most human parts of
me are those I have inhabited
and hidden from the world.
I will work on it.
I will raise my voice.
I will be heard.

But, I Don't Have Time to Practice!

Think twice before excusing yourself from practicing your speech, presentation, wedding toast, introducing your boss, or even introducing yourself. A recent survey conducted by the National Association of Colleges and Employers (NACE) found that verbal communication was the #1 skill employers were looking for when screening job candidates.[18] NACE is just one of several organizations that regularly polls employers on the skills and attributes they look for in qualified candidates. Verbal communication skills consistently rank near or at the top of each list. The option to take a detour around speaking in public is no longer in anyone's best interest. Most career professionals find themselves having to sharpen their speaking and presentation skills to get ahead. And not just once, but many times over the course of their career.

If you decide that this is the year to bring your skills to the next level, or perhaps to get up in front of a group of people for the first time and wow them with your expertise, your ideas, or the product you are trying to sell, then the most important step you can take is to find low stakes opportunities to practice your communication skills. We are constantly offered chances to speak in public, but we don't recognize them because they are dressed in the mundane camouflage of daily transactional tasks. Take a look at the top three low-stakes ways to practice your public speaking skills:

1. **Running a meeting.** Practice speaking in a succinct manner while introducing the agenda, the purpose of the meeting, and the ideal outcome you will achieve before everyone goes back to their desks. Three sentences, that when delivered in a clear and compelling manner, complete with eye contact and vocal variety, will make your co-workers wonder what just happened.

2. **Ordering from a menu.** How often do you hold up the ordering process because you don't know what you want and have a hard time getting your order out? Have you ever found yourself in line at a Qdoba or Chipotle restaurant behind a sluggish and indecisive person? It sounds like this:

   Server: "Do you want black or pinto beans?"
   Guest: "Ummmmm...pinto – No! black beans."

Server: "Pepper Jack cheese or cheddar?"

Guest: "Ummmmmm, Pepp- no wait – chedd – no, umm, is there any other kind?"

And on it goes until finally the person's burrito has reached the cashier. The next time you find yourself ordering from a menu or from a line server, narrow your focus and deliver a clear and concise order. By the way, you can do this at the drive-through as well.

3. **Leaving a voicemail message.** This is the best way to critique yourself. The next time you get someone's voicemail greeting, leave your message and then press the * key or whichever prompt the voicemail program gives you to review your message. How did you do? What can be improved? Once you have listened and made note of your less-than-stellar verbal or vocal habits, erase the message and try again. Voilà! Instant, real-world practice.

I understand that there may not always be ample time to practice your full presentation. I know that many presenters will merely scroll through their slides, review their key message points, maybe even make a final note or two, and call it a day. That works fine if your intention is to remain mediocre, or if you assume that any fumbles will be forgiven because of your busy schedule. On the other hand, if you want or need to make a better impression, then carving out the time to practice your verbal delivery, mastering your content, and getting your timing down perfectly will pay off in ways you may not even anticipate. People will see you in a new light. You are now someone to be taken more seriously. You got game!

Don't Let Mixed Signals Ruin Your Mojo

A couple of years ago I was giving a talk in a room with a faulty thermostat. When we started at 9:00 a.m. it was a bit uncomfortable. One hour into a three-hour presentation it was "Africa hot." I called the maintenance staff. I opened every door. I ordered more ice for cold drinks. I had people up out of their chairs and interacting in the hopes it would take their mind off the stifling heat. Nothing was going to resolve the situation – except to end early. If I had been at all tentative about the presentation, I could have easily concluded I was to blame for the lack of attention and dazed facial expressions. It wasn't until someone started fanning themselves that I caught on to what was happening.

As I was packing up after ending early, I thought about how many times a speaker could lose their footing by misinterpreting the signals from their audience. And that got me thinking about an audience "hierarchy of needs," much in the same way psychologist Abraham Maslow proposed in a 1943 paper entitled, *A Theory of Human Motivation*.[19] His theory is based on the premise that humans have universal needs – beginning with food, water, and shelter, and ending in self-actualization.

I came up with this back-of-the-envelope schematic below.

Level 1: If your room does not provide the **basic**s like 70-degree temperature, coffee, sugar, and comfortable seating, then you are doomed before you start. Can you address any of these issues ahead of time?

Level 2: Once the basics are covered, then the next concern for audience members is whether their **comfort zone** will be tested. Will they have to do something or say something that feels risky? For example, they may be thinking, "Will I have to catch someone as

they fall backwards?!" Offering them an overview of what to expect can do wonders for their attention span and willingness to store their iPad for the duration.

Level 3: Next up is the need to be **entertained**. OK, it's more of a wish, but it still bears mentioning. Did you include a few stories and vivid examples in your outline? Also, if you feel comfortable doing so, can you add a bit of humor to your talk? In this age of Kardashians and Situations, it pays to increase the entertainment value.

Level 4: Now we're at the social level of the audience hierarchy: the chance to find out who's in the room and to actually **get to talk conversationally,** and who knows, encounter a new prospect or customer. How can you include some sort of low stakes interaction in your presentation? Also, it pays to work out the sightlines in the room. Can everyone see you and can they see each other? Is there a support beam in the middle of the room that will determine your room set-up? Are any of the chairs sitting in darkness? All of these things will have an impact your presentation, no matter how compelling your topic.

Level 5: Every speaker, at every moment in the presentation, is battling for the attention of their audience members. In this multi-tasking, over-scheduled culture we all live in, it's more important than ever to organize your presentation around the needs of your audience and what they want to hear. If you can't afford for anyone to miss any of your message points, then it will be necessary to provide a road map right up front. It is simply no longer considered rude to get up and leave before a presenter is finished.

Meeting every need on this hierarchy cannot be practiced in your living room. You only get good at being audience-centric by focusing on it in real time.

Coaching Session

Identify five possible opportunities to speak in public within the next six months. They don't have to be formal presentations. They could be things like project updates, saying a few words at someone's birthday party, giving a toast, introducing a speaker, etc. List them here with a date next to them. Finally, decide what skill you would like to work on in each speaking opportunity. We can only achieve tangible results from what we actually measure.

Speaking Opportunity	Date/Time Frame	Performance Goal
1.		
2.		
3.		
4.		
5.		

Put an Exclamation Point on It!

One of my favorite Seinfeld episodes is the one where Elaine's boss calls her into his office to discuss her edits to a manuscript and asks her to explain all the added exclamation points. In a halting, stammering response, she tells him that the writing lacked "a certain emotion and intensity." He then tells her to go back to her office and delete them all.

I thought of this scene after sitting through a pitch meeting consisting of 15 presentations, all but two lacking in emotion and intensity. The two successful pitch teams managed to capture the panel's undivided attention. It was as if they were the only two groups that used verbal exclamation points.

The myth of work-related presentations is the presenter must be logical, analytical, and strategic and any display of emotion or optimism will be viewed as dumbed-down, pom-pom-waving fluff. Nothing could be further from the truth. As I mentioned in the last section, we all live in an "entertain-me" society, which means a presenter who is devoid of emotion or intensity makes no impression. To further illustrate this point, here is what one of the reviewers wrote about a particularly dull pitch: "No impression. Colorless."

So, how did the two presenters wow the audience? What made them stand out from the others? First, their verbal delivery was positive, assertive, and compelling. Second, their non-verbal gestures aligned with and even enhanced their words. Third, they told a story.

If you need to ask for money, get approval for your project, make a case for a promotion, or say a few words at a co-worker's going-away party, practice your delivery in two ways. First, speak in a more animated style – peppered with a few verbal exclamation points – while making eye contact with your practice audience. On the second take, deliver your remarks with less energy, no punctuation and no eye contact. Then ask your audience which one they preferred.

"Be different,
stand out,
and work your butt off."

- Reba McEntyre

Coaching Session

At the beginning of this chapter I asked you to plot your inclination toward public speaking along a continuum. Now I hope you will take a moment to honestly assess your interpersonal communication skills. Odds are that you have several attributes that effortlessly cross over to public speaking and to delivering compelling presentations. It's important to know what those are, as much as it is helpful to know where you have room to grow.

Statement	Not at all	Sometimes	Always
I rarely wait for others to initiate a conversation			
I am comfortable making small talk			
I am able to establish rapport with others			
I know how and when to end a conversation			
I regularly practice active listening			
I have a positive outlook that others pick up on			
I can accept all types of feedback			
I tend to keep my head up to engage with others			
I rarely have to ask people to repeat themselves			
I can read a room and respond accordingly			

If you placed yourself on the left-hand side of the public speaking continuum on page 45, then you would do well to find ways to incorporate your strongest interpersonal skills into your public speaking experiences. Don't settle for less than your best because you fear the limelight or you are too busy to practice. Don't let yourself off the hook because you tend to judge your abilities against an unrealistic standard. Set your expectations toward the next level up, and then the next level, and soon you will wonder why you ever doubted yourself in the first place.

Connect With Your Audience and Your Confidence Will Soar

When I was growing up, there was a framed print in our living room of President John F. Kennedy's face with a billowing American flag as a backdrop. In the bottom right corner was an image of JFK, Jr. in his little blue coat with one hand at his forehead in a military salute. That framed lithograph stayed on the same wall for years. Scant wonder that it is woven into the fabric of my childhood memories.

Without having planned any of it in advance, I happened to mention the JFK image during a presentation, and lo and behold, the majority of audience members started smiling and nodding their heads. It was like the air changed in the room. I paused and asked if there were others who had the same memory, and sure enough, people of all ages and backgrounds had a similar print in their or a relative's home. Without any fanfare or arm waving, I had made a meaningful connection with my audience. The rest of the presentation was a breeze, and I felt like I was walking on air when it was over.

To put it in more academic terms, the audience granted me a higher degree of credibility as a result of having discovered a common experience. Researchers have found that there are three types of credibility[20]:

1. **Initial credibility** – the audience's perception of the speaker *before* the speech begins
2. **Derived credibility** – resulting from everything a speaker says and does during the speech
3. **Terminal credibility** – the audience's perception of the speaker at the end of the speech

This is why connecting with your audience at the beginning of your presentation is so important. You may come into the room with a certain degree of credibility, but you benefit from building more social capital in order to achieve your purpose. If you are speaking in order to persuade, inspire, or motivate, and you feel any degree of nervousness, the best thing to do is settle into the first few minutes of the presentation. Slow down, take a breath, smile, and begin the all-important process of connecting with your audience. Most nervous speakers do the opposite. They launch themselves into the presentation at 70 mph with their head down and no recognition of the busy people sitting before them.

There is no "one way" to connect. Quite often it will depend on your topic, the type of audience, and your personality. Regardless of what approach you take, there are four important elements of connecting with others that will help any speaker break the imaginary wall:

1. **Be yourself.** The audience needs to see an authentic person up there, not an imitation of Oprah or Ellen.

2. **Resist the urge to launch into your first point.** Use your introduction – which should constitute 10-15% of your entire speech – as an opportunity to become interesting to your audience.

3. **Share something about yourself.** This is a great way to find common ground with your audience.

4. **Individualize the audience members.** A wise person once said, "Be where your feet are." The introduction is an important time to recognize and welcome your audience, as if they were walking through your front door. One easy way to do this is to make eye contact with individuals in the room, and if you find a friendly face, then you are more apt to release any tense energy. The rule of thumb is two to three seconds per person.

There's a good reason why every touring musician, singer, and comedian finds a moment early in the performance to yell out, "What's up St. Louis!" or whatever town they're in that evening. They know that establishing a connection with that particular audience through a fun, but also respectful acknowledgement of who's in the theatre, will make the rest of the night more successful and memorable for all involved.

Finding Your Confidence When You Must Speak on the Spot

At the end of every semester, I ask my graduate students what changes I could make to improve my persuasive speaking course. The #1 response – by a margin of 2 to 1 – is they want more time to practice impromptu speaking. I couldn't agree more. It's much easier to deliver a speech you wrote yourself than it is to sound intelligent and engaging on the spot.

Extemporaneous speaking is the ability to form a coherent and impactful response to a question or an invitation to comment without any prior preparation. Back in 1915, author Louis Bautain wrote a dense book on the topic entitled *The Art of Extempore Speaking*.[21] His description of what happens when we try to speak extemporaneously has yet to be improved upon:

> *"...there is as yet only a vague and shapeless product that floats upon the waters of the understanding and over which broods the spirit of life which has indeed animated it, but which has still to develop and to organize it; to give it an individuality by means of words.*
>
> *When therefore you have conceived an idea, unless it be perfectly clear to you at first glance, be in no haste to throw it into shape."*

Sage advice for anyone who gets *verklempt* when they hear someone ask, "What do you think?" or "Why is it that...?" Like any other skill, the more we practice the better we get. I have the perfect activity for you to develop your impromptu speaking abilities. Ready? Great, let's go!

"Plunge boldly into the thick of life,

and seize it where you will.

It is always interesting."

- Goethe

Coaching Session

First, invite a friend to lunch. (Look how I made impromptu speaking fun already!) Once you are seated with your favorite motivational beverage, let your friend know you would like to practice impromptu speaking in five-minute intervals. How can they say no? Have your friend choose a question from the options on the next page, and then respond for two minutes.

Why two minutes and not the whole five? Two reasons. First, brevity is key. It is important to stop speaking before your audience has either stopped listening or has loaded up a full arsenal of counter-arguments. Second, an essential feature of this activity is feedback. Use the remaining three minutes asking your friend what worked and what you can improve on. Now switch and repeat the process. Go back and forth until one of the following two things has occurred:

1. You both fall on the floor laughing and cannot finish your meal

2. You get noticeably better at impromptu speaking

How do highly-skilled speakers always sound so natural and spontaneous? They have a structure to follow. Mnemonic devices are great for making it easy to remember a multi-step format without having to bring a cheat sheet everywhere you go. Here's the one I created for my clients. Speak extemporaneously for the whole two minutes using PACE as your guide.

P – *Position*   State your belief, opinion, or judgment

A – *Analysis*   Explain why you feel this way, include facts

C – *Color*   Include examples, a personal anecdote, etc.

E – *End*   Every speech needs a strong closer. Don't just fade away, offer a clear and concise restatement of your position or main argument

Now for your fun topics

1. Who is the most confident woman you know?

2. What is it with men and golf?

3. Should Hillary Clinton run for president again?

4. What's the best movie ever made?

5. Should all Americans drive an electric car by 2020?

6. What is it about women and shopping?

7. If you found $10,000 in the street what would you do?

8. Beach house or mountain cabin?

9. Do reality TV shows like *Real Housewives* help or hurt women?

10. How do we demolish the glass ceiling for good?

The Secret to Overcoming Fear of Failure

We've all been there: that heart pounding, hands shaking, holy s+*# moment as we stand up to present, sing, debate, act, introduce someone, or even eulogize in public. And yes, we all know too much stage fright can derail a potentially great performance. But before we continue, it's important to note that a little *agita* is very helpful. It provides a sharper focus and enables our authenticity to shine through. The opposite of stage fright is not confidence. The opposite is detachment.

After a tough coaching session with a client who was spitting mad at his boss for undermining him in a meeting with an important customer, I had another Aha! Moment. I am always so grateful when these light-of-dawn (cue music) moments arise, and I formulate a thought that is not only relevant and instructional, but also energizes me to keep going. I had such a flash after noticing that 40 minutes had gone by, and he was still trying to convince me he was right and his boss was wrong. No, not wrong, dead wrong.

For my part, I tried to help him see the bigger picture and to focus on his ultimate goal, which is to get the sale. And that's when it hit me – the lesson we must all learn: instead of trying to be **right**, we should try to be of **value**. It's a completely different mindset. Being right comes from above and turns downward toward those beneath us. Being of value comes from below in a show of support or from the side with an intention to collaborate.

That's the secret to eliminating stage fright. Instead of worrying about all the things that could go wrong, think instead about the fact that you have something valuable to offer. You may be a reliable expert on your topic. You may be the most inspiring singer or poet; you may have the most important message to share and everyone who listens will be better off for having heard it. But, if you build yourself up too high in your head and start thinking you have to hit the bullseye or the whole thing is a disaster, you set yourself up for failure.

The secret sauce in a cool, calm and collected performance is to shift your mental focus from *needing* to be [fill in the blank] to *wanting* to be helpful or inspirational or knowledgeable, or even just positive.

Don't you think your listeners would appreciate it? In the inimitable words of Dr. Seuss, "You are you. Now, isn't that pleasant?"

"The human brain starts working the moment
we are born and never stops until we
stand up to speak in public."

- George Jessel

Coaching Session

Take a few moments to fill in the boxes below. The exercise is designed to redirect your thinking so that the tense energy dissipates before it builds to a panic attack. It's best to do this activity in close proximity to a presentation, a toast, a musical performance, asking for a raise, interviewing for a job, etc. On the left side, write down the things that are causing you the most anxiety. On the right side, try to re-phrase those fears into things you would like to happen.

Below the boxes is an actual example from a client who now swears by this exercise. She learned firsthand that the brain science is correct: our thoughts are the instigators, not the situation or our emotional state. Our brain is in the driver's seat and we can control our thoughts if we focus on positive, aspirational outcomes. By the way, her presentation was a huge success. High fives all around.

I Must...	I Want...

Example:

I Must...	I Want...
not embarrass my boss in front of his boss	to make a positive impression when I present to the senior leadership team
sound intelligent, logical and analytical (not my strong suit)	to provide the leadership team with several options so that they can make an informed decision
have all the answers	to be helpful and professional
not forget any data points or appear clueless	to have all the relevant information organized and at my fingertips so that I am ready for any questions they might ask

3

chapter summary | speaking in public

If this chapter were...	it would be...
a song	*Respect*, by Aretha Franklin
a movie	The King's Speech
summed up in a famous quote	*"Speech is power: speech is to persuade, to convert, to compel."* - Ralph Waldo Emerson
rolled up into one word	Passion
condensed into one piece of advice	Don't hide your talents because of a fear of public speaking. We only grow when we lean into the anxiety.

chapter 4: becoming more persuasive

*"Having to speak to the doctors in a persuasive manner sucks
the life out of me. I just want to run in the other direction."*

- Former Administrative Director,
Diagnostic Imaging

The quote above was uttered quietly to me in a recent workshop on leadership development. The woman who spoke those words was attractive, friendly, attentive, and kind – the whole package. Her smile was infectious, she gave a warm greeting to everyone who walked in the room, and she sat in the front row. In the 40 minutes I had known her, she had made a wonderful first impression. I felt myself gravitating to her.

Thus, you can imagine my surprise when she shared her true feelings about assertive communication. I was puzzled for a moment because of the vast difference between the menu and the meal, as it were. And then I remembered that I had been hearing similar stories from dozens of other women. When faced with a situation that makes us feel uncomfortable, we women tend to second-guess ourselves. We let the discomfort of the moment cloud our judgment and after several bouts with this kind of thinking, we get really good at it.

Whether it's a need to be perfect or the committee in our head that exists only to question our aptitude, we have a knack for limiting our growth and development. Imagine sitting at a fork in the road. The road sign on the left says "This way to fear of failure and crippling self-doubt. The road sign on the right says "Risky and unknown, but you're very likely to reach your destination." Without even being aware of it, we turn left.

What is it that made this particular woman want run in the other direction when she had to consult with a doctor? When I asked her this question, she said that her style of communication was so timid and reserved that whenever she found herself in conversation with an assertive and busy M.D., she would instantly doubt her ability to command the situation.

We then discussed the difference between persuasion and influence, which is helpful to share here so that the upcoming strategies and coaching sessions will make more sense. Harking back to your biology class, you can think of influence as the genus and persuasion as the species. Sound familiar? Anyone? Bueller? In other words, persuasion is one aspect of influence. When we persuade, we are really trying to win the hearts and minds of our listeners. In order to do that, it helps to be seen as an influential person. The good news is you need no formal authority or fancy title to be influential.

Let's clear up the distinction between persuasion and influence. Here are the dictionary definitions:

> *Persuade: v.,* to move by argument, entreaty, or expostulation to a belief, position, or course of action

> *Influence, n.,* the act of producing an effect without exertion of force or command, to affect or alter by indirect or intangible means

For the purpose of this chapter, think of it this way: influence is silent and persuasion requires words.

To Persuade Them You Must First "WOO" Them

WOO stands for Winning Others Over. People who are gifted at WOO are likeable, helpful, have a genuine interest in others, and of course, are persuasive. In conducting research for their book *The Art of WOO: Using Strategic Persuasion to Sell Your Ideas,* Richard Shell and Mario Moussa found that the ability to persuade is a strong predictor of performance ratings of employees, often outstripping both intelligence and personality traits.[22] People with strong social skills command higher fees and salaries than equally talented, but less socially adept colleagues. People with a healthy dose of WOO play good politics at work, and they understand that no one else can take responsibility for *their* career advancement.

Let me share a client success story to illustrate this point. Jessica is the manager of a call center for a large online retailer. She is a quiet problem-solver, well-liked by her co-workers and her staff, but was recently passed over for a promotion because her boss said she wasn't ready. This is where I came in because Jessica decided to work with a coach so that she could be better prepared when the next opportunity for promotion came around.

I started out by trying to identify the reasons why her boss felt she wasn't ready (could he have been any less vague?). I learned that she hesitated to speak up in staff meetings, let her colleagues make all the recommendations for improvements and take all the credit for good results, and she never officially asked for the promotion. In a nutshell, Jessica has trouble standing out in the crowd. Like thousands of other capable women, Jessica operates from the premise that consistent quality performance is all it takes to get ahead, i.e., let the work speak for itself. What a nice concept. Too bad it's insufficient. It's the career equivalent of clapping with one hand.

Because I much prefer to focus on tangible steps my clients can take to achieve their goals, I asked her two questions that launched us into devising a plan of action. I first wanted to know if there were other people in the organization who could vouch for her readiness to move to the next level. She said yes and named three people who played significant roles in the organization. It turned out one of them was a senior vice president of the company. Good for her.

The second question was whether there were any opportunities in the next few months to enhance her reputation as an up-and-coming leader in the organization. I suspected Jessica was not seen as influential or persuasive. If I was right, she was going to need to make a case for this promotion, and since her boss was sending a very clear message that he was unwilling to invest his time or energy in helping her prepare for the next level, then she had to become her own champion.

Jessica told me that because of the success of her call center, she was invited to the annual meeting at which all three people she mentioned would be in attendance. We got to work on preparing for this meeting. We role-played conversations with each person and talked about how she could advocate for herself without grandstanding, which turned out to be the root cause of her inhibitions in meetings. We talked about the difference between good and bad politics in the workplace, about managing up and across, and about the role confidence would play in achieving her goal of being promoted within the year. We even discussed what she should wear. Off she went to the meeting.

There are many aspects to this story I find so relevant to this book, but suffice it to say that Jessica worked the annual meeting like a celebrity on the red carpet. She socialized, contributed to discussions, and when appropriate, she sang the praises of her team back home. She also spoke with all three of her go-to people. Oh yes she did! The most exciting outcome for Jessica was the conversation with the senior vice president who said, "You've done really good work this year, Jessica, and we hope you will be with us at next year's meeting." Jessica not only received her promotion, but she earned it as well.

"Your projects, programs, and career turn on the difference between 'no' and 'yes.' Yet selling ideas– especially the kinds of ideas that make organizations work–is a skill shrouded in mystery. Part emotional intelligence, part politics, part rhetoric, and part psychology, selling ideas is not like tricking someone out of his money. It's about helping others to see things your way by engaging their minds and imaginations."

- Richard Shell and Mario Moussa, *The Art of Woo*

Coaching Session

Do you want to or need to become more persuasive? Do you want to make a better case for yourself at work or in your relationship? As my friend Felicia would say, do you need to get your agency back? Then the best place to start is with Shell and Moussa's four questions (I have altered them slightly to be more broadly applicable).

What is your natural communication style? Are you more on the passive side, characterized by fear of upsetting others? Perhaps you tend toward the aggressive side characterized by a more directive, self-serving approach that can sometimes alienate others. Or are you more balanced and capable of assertive communication, characterized by an awareness of the needs of others as well as your own and trying to find a workable solution for all?

Be honest with yourself as you try to plot your style on this continuum:

Passive	Assertive	Aggressive
I lose/you win.	I win/ you win.	I win/you lose.
Resist taking action or confronting others	Concern for self as well as for others	Not aware of needs of others; tries to control the decision/outcome

Who are you trying to persuade and what's on their mind? What do they care about?

Are your interests aligned or conflicting?

What is the default style of communication in your organization/your relationship? Examples: Direct/Indirect? Focused/Distracted? Clear/Unclear? Timely/Delayed?

What, at this moment, is the optimal approach?

The Six Core Elements of Persuasion

So now you have wooed your boss, lover, spouse, or neighbor and you are ready to persuade them to your way of thinking. The next step is to use the right tool for the job. Measure twice, cut once.

University of Arizona Professor Robert Cialdini has spent his career studying the art and craft of persuasion. He has culled an extensive array of research findings into six, easily digestible factors that he calls the Six Elements of Persuasion.[23] They are:

1. **Reciprocity** – The most common use of this concept is free samples. Whole Foods uses this technique every Saturday with its sampling stations in the hopes you'll march right over to the shelf and pick up a bottle of the artisanal cranberry pumpkin white balsamic vinegar. The idea comes down to this: if you want me to do something, think something, buy something, then you go first.

2. **Social Proof** – When we feel hesitant about a particular course of action we will look to those around us to guide our decisions and actions. What group of people has the most influence on our choices? Our peer group. Cialdini cites the TV laugh track as the very definition of social proof.

3. **Commitment and Consistency** – As a general rule, human beings do not like to back out of deals or commitments (hence the name of this book!). Cialdini's research has found that we are more likely to do something after we've agreed to it verbally or in writing. One small, but important caveat: this behavior becomes more prevalent as we get older. So don't go trying this on a 15-year-old and expecting amazing results.

4. **Likeability** – People tend to give more credence to those whom they like and respect. Cialdini goes on to say that we are also more likely to favor those who are physically attractive, similar to ourselves, or who offer compliments. We look for similarities and when we find them, we ascribe positive qualities to the other person.

5. **Authority** – As a general rule, we respect authority (again, teenagers can be the exception). We want to follow the lead of people we believe are genuine experts. This is why up-talking, mitigated speech and hesitation can sap your credibility.

   Note: Cialdini's research shows that even the appearance of authority can boost our ability to persuade. What's the takeaway? Well, it's twofold: Go ahead and buy that killer suit at Nordstrom and, when in doubt, act as if.

6. **Scarcity** – My least favorite. This technique is used way too often to manipulate and deceive. Anyone who has ever driven by a furniture store and seen a huge sign that says "Liquidation! Everything must go! 50% off while supplies last!" knows all about the scarcity technique. It's based on supply and demand. The less available something is, the more valuable it is. Sometimes it's a legitimate claim. After all, there are only so many Beyonce or Springsteen tickets. Other times it is blatant manipulation. Be careful using this strategy.

So...How Credible Are You?

I attended a workshop with Edward Tufte who is best known as the guru of persuading with data.[24] Toward the end of the daylong seminar, Tufte offered helpful advice to anyone needing to persuade: "You are ready to persuade when you can write 250 words on the problem, the relevance, and the solution."

He went on to say that only with deliberate self-awareness of one's own expertise can a person ever expect someone to pay close attention. Let me repeat that: *deliberate self-awareness* of one's own expertise. He suggests that there are only two elements to a persuasive presentation:

   1. Tell your story

   2. Make your audience believe you

Most people who attempt to persuade others tend to fall on opposite ends of the spectrum. We either minimize our expertise because we don't want to appear superior, or we make everything so over-wrought and complicated that no one listens long enough to hear our recommendation. If we spent some time figuring out what our audience needs to know in order to believe what we say, we might actually get the job, promotion, or the new customer.

One piece of advice I received early on that has enhanced my ability to persuade is to avoid talking in superlatives. In other words, show, don't tell. No one really cares if you are the smartest, the most creative, or "world class." With that kind of self-promotion you might as well be wearing a NASCAR uniform covered with a hundred different logos.

Instead, our focus should be on the listener. We should be learning what their needs are and what keeps them up at night, and then we can do what everyone is hoping for: we can try to solve their problem. Give them an answer to the "What's in it for me?" question every human being has running on a continuous loop.

Unless you have reached a point in your career or relationship at which you no longer need to explain the rationale for your position, then do yourself and your audience a huge favor by spending quality time mulling over your answer to the following question: why should we listen to you?

Three Ways to Inspire *and* Persuade

I was meeting with a new client recently to get an idea of what she was hoping to achieve from our work together. She said quite simply, "I *want* to be more inspiring and I *have* to be more persuasive. The first part is for my personal growth and the second part is for my job." Immediately an image popped into my head of a time when I was both inspired *and* persuaded.

It happened at a large conference of business leaders and education reformers who had gathered to discuss the then radical notion of charter schools and whether they were just a nefarious scheme to rob existing schools of precious resources, or the elixir for all that ails public education. The stakes were high, lines were drawn, and emotions were palpable.

The keynote speaker at this conference was Dr. Howard Fuller, former Superintendent of Milwaukee Public Schools and currently Director of the Center for the Transformation of Learning at Marquette University. He not only captured the hearts and minds of everyone in the room, but he persuaded many skeptics that charters were worthy of a second look. He used the concept of educational equity as a way to establish common ground and he let his passion for the topic shine through. He was also successful in articulating *why* the audience should care about the charter school movement. Not from his point of view, but from theirs.

Part preacher, part storyteller, with a little in-your-face poetry slam technique thrown in for good measure, Howard Fuller blends the qualities of a captivating speaker and artful persuader into one powerful delivery. Since I took notes that day, I can share with you the three verbal techniques he used to earn the rapt attention of his audience.

Kinesthetic Imagery. Creating the feeling of motion, movement, or muscular tension/relaxation.

"What I have learned over the years is that far too many of us support change as long as nothing changes. Change is hard. At every level it's hard. And as soon as you get some traction, someone will ask, 'Why are we doing this? Can't we go back to the old way?' So I started this mantra of 'leap before you look.' Because if you look too long, you will never leap. You'll be standing over that cliff, looking out, and waiting, and waiting some more. But if you jump, you discover that there is an urgency to find new answers."

"We have rules and regulations and policies for everything. I mean EV-ry-thing. We have policies that allow adults to stay in their [school] building just because they've been there the longest. We've got people in these buildings who've been sitting back with their

arms folded for the last ten years! Peter Drucker said, 'There is nothing so useless as doing efficiently that which should not be done at all.'"

Word Repetition. Using the same word or words at the beginning of successive phrases, clauses, or sentences.

"One of the things I did was to require that all 9th graders take Algebra. You would have thought I asked for the world to end. The change blockers said, 'They're all gonna flunk!' Now, I've visited classrooms where kids were taking Math for Life, Math for Going to the Supermarket, Math for How to Get on the Bus, Math for the Living Dead. So my response was, 'If you're flunking them anyway, why not flunk them in a course that actually means something!'"

"We need people who respect our children, but I'm going to take it further and say that we need people who love our children. Because if you cannot love them, you cannot understand them. And if you cannot understand them, you cannot reach them. And if you cannot reach them, then how in the world can you expect to teach them?"

Analogy. Comparing two things for the purpose of explaining or clarifying an idea.

"Those of you who have been in an Apple store, you know there are lots of gadgets and work tables and bean bag chairs. Invariably there are kids sitting on those chairs working on computers. Now, when those kids show up in the classroom, do you think they're gonna sit in perfect rows and be quiet and turn to page four in the textbook? If you think that, you are sorely mistaken. It's like trying to teach the hip-hop generation with a waltz mentality, and then blaming the kids when it doesn't work.

So, it's not about 'schools' any more. It's about learning environments. We gotta understand that we got to change our whole way of thinking about school. All of the structures are set up to make kids successful in the 20th century. The problem is...we're in the 21st century. We've got to be in turnaround mode.

We got kids takin' care of their siblings, who could be getting a medal just for coming to school. The real problem is that the older we get the more angelic our youth becomes. And so we don't want to change because the old way worked for us. We already know more than we will ever need to know to accomplish this task. Whether or not we do it is dependent upon how we feel about the fact that we have not done it so far."

Were you moved by any of Dr. Fuller's words? If so, then you are more likely to consider his position. We cannot persuade others on the bigger issues if we do not get them to feel either the pain of doing nothing or the pleasure that will come from taking action. Certainly you can convince someone to try a new restaurant based solely on your opinion, but if you want to convince your spouse or significant other that it's time for you to quit your job even though you don't have another one lined up, then you will need more tools in your toolbox.

It takes time to cultivate the skills of persuasion and influence primarily because it involves shifting your focus from your own needs and wants to those of your audience. We are all so busy and distracted we fail to carve out the time to carefully craft a project update for our boss; request a new deadline from our project manager; or how the family should spend this year's tax refund. Our focus is on self-preservation (just let me get through this) or, in some cases, political positioning (all I need to do is get my way). We end up giving nothing of ourselves. As a result, our delivery is often dull and full of verbal junk food, taking twice as long to say, and focused on our needs instead of theirs.

If your reputation matters, then be sure to find the time to craft your argument from the other person's perspective. Then practice your delivery. Suddenly, your intention to be more persuasive has momentum. And one last word on moving others to action from one of the most persuasive leaders, Winston Churchill: "Before you can inspire others with emotion, you must first be swamped with it yourself."

More Fun with Persuasion and Confidence-building

Some persuasion techniques can be so over-used they run right off the rails. One example that comes to mind is the often-ridiculed Cialis commercial with the couple lounging in the twin bathtubs holding hands like a Michelangelo fresco painting, against a backdrop of a beautiful sunset. Really? This is the best you got?

Madison Avenue advertising firms have spent decades thinking up new ways to persuade us to part with our hard-earned money. Just look! It's new _and_ improved Tide! The following techniques are some of the more tried and true (and less nefarious) methods for becoming more persuasive. Be sure to practice these techniques in the safety of your own home or office and then bring them out into the light of day with the same success Don Draper and Peggy Olson have on _Mad Men_.

1. **Experts.** Can you think of anyone whose knowledge, opinion or experience can help with the veracity of your position? The most famous example of this might be the "Four out of five doctors choose Crest for their own family" commercial.

2. **Remove Barriers.** Can you come up with any examples of how going along with your preferred plan would make life easier, more satisfying, and less time consuming? For example, I combined 1 and 2 and with great success when I coached a woman through an 80-pound weight loss – and this was before the Biggest Loser so I did not have the benefit of Cialdini's social proof. I first lined up a nutritionist to offer timely advice on how to adjust her diet. Then, acting as her personal trainer I scheduled her appointments at times that worked with her schedule. Before long, the weight was melting off.

3. **Charm and Allure.** Have you ever heard the old adage, "It's not what you say, it's how you say it"? A great thing about persuasion is it's not just about the words you choose. If you are capable of being charismatic or charming, you will be much more effective. Even good manners can pay off. After all, no one likes a whiner.

4. **Framing.** Imagine working on a jigsaw puzzle without the box cover. The picture of the puzzle is your frame. When you frame your topic you are attempting to get the other person to see the issue from your perspective. You are trying to focus their attention in a way that helps your cause. Some experts say this is a skill all leaders must acquire in order to be successful.

5. **Timing.** This is perhaps the most important aspect of being other-oriented in your approach to persuasion so that you avoid hearing the phrase, "You're bringing this up _now_?!" One glaring

example of this is the jarring reaction people have when they walk into a store the day after Halloween and see Christmas decorations.

Before you launch into your persuasive argument because you feel the need to discuss it now, ask yourself if there is a better time to have the conversation. Let's revisit Jessica's situation to fully understand the value of this particular persuasion tactic. When she came back from the annual meeting we discussed both the timing and the approach she would take to ask for a promotion should it not be forthcoming.

She decided to quietly pose the idea of a promotion to her boss a month before her annual performance review. This would allow him time to fully consider his position, and it would give her time to practice a persuasive argument if it turned out he wasn't ready to promote her. Turns out that was not necessary. She was offered the promotion based on her efforts to be a more assertive leader and take an active role in meetings.

Do You Have "Centers of Influence?"

The age-old advice "It's not what you know it's who you know" is even more relevant in this era of hash tags, tweets, likes and comments. Social media has changed the definition of an influencer. Now one of your friends on Facebook can "like" Country Outfitters and it will show up on your wall. I never even knew there was such a store and now I feel like I have to check out those cowboy boots. I didn't even know I wanted a pair of cowboy boots.

Back in the dark ages, when a tweet was the sound a bird made, you were only a center of influence (COI) if you were extremely successful in your job, if people turned to you for advice, and if no Rolodex was big enough to hold all your contacts. (For those of you who have grown up with cell phones and have never seen a Rolodex, ask your great uncle Ralph to show you – I am almost positive he will still have a rolodex on his desk somewhere.)

The COI principle is based on the notion that we are persuaded by individuals who we think are accomplished, experienced, and well-connected. For example, if you wanted to learn to downhill ski and you had the choice of getting advice from Super-G Alpine gold medalist Lyndsey Vonn or the cashier at Acme Sporting Goods, who would you choose? Exactly.

At the core of building centers of influence is mutual trust. Having moved five times in 13 years, I have benefited from this concept several times. Instead of flying blind, I have asked a female colleague for the name of a good doctor; my new neighbor who is a wealth management advisor for the name of a good accountant; and a friendly person at the dog park for the name of a good dog walker. In each case I felt I could trust the person's opinion, and they would not steer me in the wrong direction. Without trust, there is no COI.

"Aerodynamically the bumble bee
shouldn't be able to fly.
But the bumble bee doesn't know that
so it goes on flying anyway."

- Mary Kay Ash,
Founder, Mary Kay Cosmetics

Coaching Session

Take a moment and try to think of people in your world whom you would consider a COI. How have they helped you in your career or perhaps just navigating your personal life a little better? Now consider the extent to which *you* are a COI for someone else. In what ways do you perform this role? In what ways does this role generate feelings of self-worth?

Take a look at the following four elements of a COI and decide where you stand. First assess the centers of influence you have access to and whether you can answer yes to all four items. Then look at the elements through the lens being a COI for others.

How to Benefit From Your COIs	Y	N
I always avoid over-reaching. Ask for one thing at a time as opposed to a laundry list of requests.		
I am clear on the outcome I am looking for. Let your COI know exactly how they can help you.		
I always align my "ask" with the COI's sphere of influence. Would you ask a tourist for directions?		
I never take advantage of my COIs. Always express your appreciation and always stay in touch.		

Now take a moment to assess your ability to act as a Center of Influence for people in your network.

Best Practices for Acting as a COI for Others	Y	N
I am viewed as approachable. Convey to others you are willing to help in any way you can.		
I loop back in a timely manner. Reliable COIs don't let too much time lapse between requests and action.		
I never mislead people about my ability to deliver. Never say yes to a request that is outside of your sphere of influence.		
I never offer help with strings attached. True influencers never make their assistance contingent upon how others can help them.		

Next, take a moment to get in touch with your ability to be influential. I created the following self-assessment after attending a workshop run by the late Mel Silberman who was a pioneer in active learning.

Scoring instructions: For each item, place a check mark in the box that best corresponds to your skill level. When you are finished, add up your score.

Item	1 Weak	2 Fair	3 Good	4 Excellent
I establish rapport with people before trying to persuade them.				
I first try to understand the other person's point of view.				
I give compelling reasons for adopting my viewpoint.				
I'm not afraid of rejection.				
I bolster my argument with good examples.				
I present my ideas in an upbeat, positive way.				
I am sincere rather than manipulative.				
I am persistent without being a nag.				
I give people time to mull over what I've presented.				
When giving advice I avoid saying "You should..."				

What your score might say about your ability to influence others:

If you scored between 30 and 40: You see yourself as having strong, effective influence skills – right up there with Tony Soprano!

If you scored between 20 and 30: You are able to make some effort to influence others, but it often feels uncomfortable. You would rather use telepathy.

If you scored between 10 and 20: Influencing is not your thing. You prefer to let things evolve without ruffling any feathers. Is this the best approach to achieving your goals?

4

chapter summary | becoming more persuasive

If this chapter were...	it would be...
a song	*Give Me One Reason*, by Tracy Chapman
a movie	Norma Rae
summed up in a famous quote	*"Your passion for a subject will save you."* - William James
rolled up into one word	Power
condensed into one piece of advice	It's not about being stubborn or getting your way, it's about being strategic in order to achieve your goals.

chapter 5: enhancing your personal brand

"A brand is an emotional aftertaste. Think about your grandmother. Feel it? That feeling is your grandma's brand."

- Zetrank

Have you ever met someone at a party or networking event and noticed he or she had such a magnetic personality that you found yourself drawn to them? Perhaps you thought about him or her the next day. Now imagine this person is you. Being able to communicate your authentic self – your personal brand – is an essential element of confidence. Knowing who you are and what you offer the world is one half of the equation. The other half is that others see the same thing, too.

The term personal branding first appeared in a *Fast Company*[25] article by Tom Peters in which he wrote,

"Regardless of age, regardless of position, regardless of the business we happen to be in, all of us need to understand the importance of branding. We are CEOs of our own companies: Me Inc. To be in business today, our most important job is to be head marketer for the brand called You."

Effective and enduring personal brands do the important job of differentiating you from the pack. A brand can help you stand out in your area of expertise, among job candidates, or among twenty pairs of flip flops. Your brand is a fusion of your personal values, your skills, your passion, and your purpose. After you have experimented with various recipes and your brand is "fully baked," you can enjoy the benefits of a consistently vivid and identifiable aftertaste – much like Chanel No. 5.

Here comes the tough love: you can only experience the benefits of a strong personal brand if you are willing to put in the work. That work includes honest reflection, self-assessment, strengths-finding, and a commitment to manifest the results in your everyday interactions with others. What's worse than a sour "emotional aftertaste" is one that lacks any flavor whatsoever. In this chapter we will explore the concept of developing a personal brand and the steps to take to identify the core elements that comprise your unique brand. But first I want to connect this topic to chapter 1: cultivating personal presence. It's less about the circular argument of what comes first, and more about the fact that these two concepts go hand-in-hand. Genuine presence leads to a strong personal brand. Let me explain by sharing a real-life example.

I've been working with a cross-functional team recently and I had the pleasure of sitting in on their big presentation to the organization's senior leaders. It was thrilling to watch their respective bosses sit up, open their eyes, nod their heads, and take copious notes. The team succeeded in getting the senior leaders to approve their recommendations. The success was largely based on one particular team member who possesses a strong personal presence and who is now being cultivated for a leadership position.

That team member, we'll call her Sarah, made a much stronger impression on the audience than did her counterparts. As Nancy Duarte would say, Sarah resonated.[26] She had an effect on people that went beyond the verbal transaction. She built her credibility through genuine connection. During the Q&A segment, she was called upon twice as often as her fellow teammates. None of it was rocket science or some Vulcan mind meld, but rather good old fashioned chemistry. Based on my observations, I offer the following advice for anyone wanting to make a significant, positive impact on others.

1. **Operate on all cylinders.** The other presenters hid behind the laptop, spoke in a procedural manner with their heads turned toward the screen, and their hands folded in the fig leaf position. By contrast, Sarah stepped toward the audience before she started, smiled, used her hands, and let the audience know she wanted to be there, speaking to them, about matters of importance. I noticed a few people put their iPads and cell phones aside when Sarah was speaking.

2. **Don't be boring.** Sarah started out with a few left-brain items to demonstrate the team had done their research, but she didn't stop

there. To engage her audience even more, she switched to the right side, the emotional side of the brain. She helped the audience feel something by painting a picture of what life would be like when all of the team's recommendations were implemented. Moving an audience to action takes more than logic.

3. Take the temperature of the room. Sarah was the only presenter who "read the room." At one point she gave her team a silent signal to stop the presentation in order to generate discussion. It was exactly what the leadership team wanted. Just because you have ten more slides left does not mean you should barrel through all ten slides.

4. Strike a balance. The average audience can pick up on the speaker's internal state of mind. If you are operating on two cylinders, or you have blinders on, your listeners can sense this and they decide that you are not worth their time or attention. Personal presence requires an alignment between your internal state and your outward expression. The schematic below shows the balancing act required to project magnetic personal presence. Successful people – whether they are hugely popular extroverts who love the stage, or dependable, respected introverts who prefer small group settings – all manage to strike a balance between awareness of others and their surroundings, and feeling truly at ease.

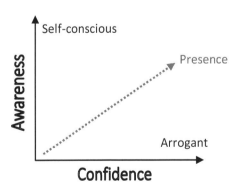

Using any of the above strategies will enhance your personal brand. You will leave a unique and pleasant aftertaste wherever you go. Applying all four of these techniques effectively and consistently will enhance your career.

How Do You Cultivate a Personal Brand?

This is not a trivial question. And that's not me talking, that's Norm Smallwood and Dave Ulrich, co-authors of the Harvard Management Newsletter article entitled *Five Steps to Developing Your Leadership Brand*.[27] Here is their definition of a personal brand:

> *"A personal brand allows all that's powerful and effective about [you] to become known to [others], enabling you to generate maximum value."*

What I have found most effective in coaching clients through the development of their personal brand is once they get clear on the core aspects of their identity, they become more energized and motivated to go out and use it to maximum effect. Why? Because as Smallwood and Ulrich have found in their research, when you clearly identify what you want to be known for, it is easier to let go of the things that keep your brand hidden from others. Instead, you start to concentrate on the activities that bring it into the light of day. In essence, you work smarter, not harder.

Now is the time to start thinking like a celebrity who hires a team of people to create and sustain a certain public persona. As one of my clients said, "I don't want to be vanilla. I'm much more interesting than that." And she is. She just hadn't devoted the time or energy to figure out what constitutes "interesting" and what steps she should take to ensure other people consistently pick up on it.

Over the next several pages you will have the opportunity to delve into the five steps. Don't rush through them. Do your best to fully consider your answers so that when you're finished, you will have identified your trademark. As Oscar Wilde once said, "Be yourself. Everyone else is taken."

One other note: while the original version of these steps focused on career and leadership development, I have made some adjustments in language to include your non-work life and/or your social life if that is where your focus is right now. So grab a pen, put on your thinking cap and dive in.

Coaching Session

Step #1: What results do you want to achieve in the next year?

In the next 12 months, what are the major results you want to achieve at work, in your career, or your life as whole? To get at those results, take a look at the following ten groups of people and identify those groups whose interests you want to consider as you identify your intended results.

Colleagues	Supervisor(s)
Friends	Family members
Employees	Customers
Students	Teachers/Professors
Recruiters	Voters

Results:

1. _____
2. _____
3. _____
4. _____
5. _____

Look back on what you wrote and be sure that you have only included major goals. If any of the intended results do not fall into that category, cross them out. It's important to think big. This is not a To Do list. There should be no more than five, and three really good ones might be more attainable. Remember, time flies when you're having fun. Too many goals mean your attention will be spread too thin.

Now that you have your list of intended results you are ready for the next step.

Question #2: What do you wish to be known for?

Using the following list of adjectives, choose six words that capture the essence of your personality, your values, or your beliefs. You only want words that get at the essence of you. Do not feel limited to this list of words. Feel free to use other words that best capture the essence of how you wish to be perceived. Limit yourself to only six words so that you do not dilute your brand.

Analytical	Approachable	Assertive	Optimistic
Attentive	Benevolent	Bold	Organized
Bright	Calm	Caring	Outgoing
Charismatic	Clever	Collaborative	Passionate
Committed	Compassionate	Competent	Patient
Concerned	Confident	Consistent	Personable
Conscientious	Considerate	Decisive	Polite
Creative	Curious	Dependable	Positive
Dedicated	Deliberate	Disciplined	Respectful
Determined	Diplomatic	Efficient	Responsible
Driven	Easygoing	Enthusiastic	Satisfied
Emotional	Energetic	Flexible	Savvy
Even-tempered	Fast	Friendly	Selfless
Focused	Forgiving	Happy	Sincere
Fun-loving	Good listener	Hopeful	Thorough
Helpful	Honest	Innovative	Thoughtful
Humble	Independent	Logical	Tireless
Insightful	Inspired	Loyal	Trustworthy
Intelligent	Inventive	Loving	Warm
Kind	Knowledgeable	Nurturing	Witty

3. Define your identity

Now comes the challenging part. You'll need to take your time and let the creative, right side of your brain take over. Your next task is to combine your six words into three, two-word phrases that reflect your true identity. This exercise allows you to build a deeper, more complex description: not only what you want to be known for, but how you will probably have to act to get there. For example, calmly driven differs from tirelessly driven. Experimenting with several combinations of your six chosen words will help you crystallize your personal brand.

To help get your creative juices flowing, here are three choices made by one of my career coaching clients who was preparing for a series of job interviews.

Cooperatively-driven   Warmly-scrutinizing   Patiently-demanding

Try to fill in all six spaces here and then choose your final three.

_____	-	_____
_____	-	_____
_____	-	_____
_____	-	_____
_____	-	_____
_____	-	_____

4. Construct your brand statement (motto), then test it.

In this step, you are attempting to pull everything together into a declarative, even catchy statement that makes a "so that" connection between what you want to be known for (Steps 2 and 3) and your desired results (Step 1). If you have completed all the coaching sessions up until this point, you may have good content already written down on pages 29, 32, and 40 that will help you fill in the blanks:

I want to be known for being _____

so that I can deliver _____.

Smallwood and Ulrich offer this example of a brand statement from one of their clients: "I want to be known for being independently innovative, deliberately collaborative and strategically results-oriented so that I can deliver superior financial outcomes for my business."

You don't have to use all of your two-word phrases as the example shows. Your statement is easier to remember – and to measure – if you can boil it down to its essence.

Re-write your brand statement, or your personal commercial, one more time in the space below:

_____

_____

_____

Now test the veracity of the statement by asking yourself the following questions:

> Does this statement represent who I am and what I can do?   Y_ N_

> Will it help me unlock my full potential and value to others?   Y_ N_

> Will this brand be received positively by others?   Y_ N_

> Am I able to consistently express this brand?   Y_ N_

5. Now make your brand identity real

You have reached a critical point in the personal brand development process: being willing to fully commit to your statement. It is now important to find ways to manifest your brand in your daily life. One way to do this is to share your statement and two-word phrases with your friends, colleagues, even your boss. Ask them if they see you as you wish to be seen. If you say you are flexible and approachable, do others experience you in that way?

The exercise of forging a personal brand and the day-to-day discipline of making it real can help you stay focused on the most important challenges you encounter. For example, my "warmly-scrutinizing" client was often tested in her effort to maintain a congenial manner when observing mistakes made by her bank teller staff.

No personal brand is static. Rather, your brand should evolve in response to the different expectations you face at different times in your life. The only thing more important than having a personal brand is keeping it fluid so that it continues to serve your needs as you encounter new challenges and situations.

As we wrap up this chapter, I hope you are convinced that building a compelling personal brand is worth the effort. You may still be mulling it over. You may find yourself pondering the question, "Does a strong personal brand really matter that much?" Allow me to answer that question definitively: It only matters on the days of the week that end in y.

As the song goes, "the knee bone's connected to the thigh bone. The thigh bone's connected to the back bone." And so on. Your branding efforts are directly connected to your personal, social, and career success. The more effort you apply to identifying and then manifesting your unique qualities, the more results you will achieve.

Over the past month, I have conducted a series of telephone interviews for one of my leadership coaching clients. We'll call her Donna. I have spoken with seven individuals who know her well. I can now report back to Donna that she has developed a distinctive emotional aftertaste. Every person described her as hard-working, focused, detail-oriented, and having a great sense of humor. That's the good news – and I will encourage her to use these adjectives to create her two-word phrases.

The bad news is there is also a noticeable downside to her brand (what a shock to discover that Donna is human). Our work together will focus largely on the ways in which she can further develop her positive attributes while minimizing the negative. As I mentioned in the beginning of this chapter, personal branding takes effort, reflection, and energy to maintain a brand that works in service of your goals rather than impeding them. I already know this coaching engagement will result in positive outcomes for Donna and for her organization. Why? Because Donna has plenty of grit – Seligman's essential element of well-being (see page 31). She will do the hard work necessary to improve her brand. She already knows she has value and she's proud of her contributions. It is this very awareness – this positive sense of self – that will help her improve her personal brand.

5

chapter summary | enhancing your personal brand

If this chapter were...	it would be...
a song	*All Systems Go* by Donna Summer
a movie	Invictus
summed up in a famous quote	*"You are unique. No one can tell you how to use your time. It is yours. Your life is your own. You mold it. You make it."* - Eleanor Roosevelt
rolled up into one word	Distinction
condensed into one piece of advice	Authenticity is more valuable than expertise.

putting it all together

"The future depends on what we do in the present."

- Mahatma Gandhi

I was sitting in a Starbucks near a college campus one day last fall, and I overheard a conversation between a male private equity manager and a female MBA student. He had volunteered to help students practice their pitch before they were to do it live at the annual Angel Investor's conference.

The student was sitting in the chair with her legs pulled up, arms wrapped around her shins, chin resting on her knees, and her hair draped over the right side of her face. She could not have taken up any less cubic space. By contrast, the equity manager was sitting back in his chair, feet splayed, hands clasped behind his head – the classic alpha male pose. His body language said, "Pay attention to me 'cuz I'm smart, and I'm rich." Hers said, "Don't look at me because I'm nervous and unsure of myself."

She must have already pitched her business idea because the table was strewn with paper, and he was giving her direct feedback. He said, "You've got to understand that accounting and production mean nothing to me until I know what value your idea has for you. Why do *you* care about it? That gives me a reason why *I* should care." She responded by saying something in a tiny, squeaky voice about having resolved all the production issues which made the plan more feasible. Unfortunately, she had a terrible habit of up-talking so it sounded like a question – full of doubt and lacking conviction.

The equity manager was becoming frustrated. It was clear he wanted her to be more assertive and confident. He barked at her, "It's not about the plan! Stop telling me about the plan! If it's as doable as you say it is, then I could go into production tomorrow. This is what I do for a living. What I need from you is more assurance that your venture is the one I should invest in. I want to see that you have confidence in your idea. We've been at this for 30 minutes, and you have yet to show me that. If this were your real pitch my answer would be no."

And there it was again. The word confidence. And here I was again, witnessing a super-smart and talented woman undermine herself. It took a lot of willpower on my part not to walk over to her and ask if she wanted my help, but I could imagine her saying, "No thanks, I'm getting all the 'help' I can handle for one day." As painful as it was to hear the equity manager's feedback, I am quite sure her pitch was more effective for having done the dry run with him. What I can't know is whether her body language was any better. If it wasn't, then she sent the wrong signals. Her silent message would have screamed, "Don't look at me and don't take me seriously."

Approachability is the key to communicating your confidence to others, and to a positive first impression. When people feel comfortable approaching you, they tend to ascribe positive qualities to you before any words are exchanged. Truly confident people are in a state of relaxed readiness, no matter what comes their way. Relaxed and ready people are more likely to have great posture, are comfortable in their own skin, keep their eyes up and focused on those around them, and are apt to be smiling. All of these compelling attributes lead to higher levels of personal presence, which then lead to a more compelling personal brand.

One of my favorite books is *Acting On Stage and Off* by Robert Barton.[29] He offers helpful advice and practical tips for the aspiring actor that are equally applicable to everyday confidence building. For example, Barton offers a great definition of relaxed readiness:

> "If you are too relaxed, you fall asleep. If you are too ready, you can explode. The actor seeks a balance between ease and eagerness, between indifference and anxiety. Concentrate only on relaxation and your performance is likely to come up short on energy, vitality, clarity and power. At the other end of the extreme is locker-room frenzy, which works for sprinting and high-decibel rock, but leads to acting that burns out quickly, to performance minus nuance, shading and variety."

Let's do a quick awareness check. Think back over the last month and recall the number of times a stranger made eye contact, said hello, asked you for help, or smiled at you. If your answer is fewer than five times, then you are using your cell phone in public way too often. If your answer is eight to 12 then you are capable of letting strangers into your orbit in certain situations. If your answer was more than 12 then you are a people magnet, and have probably said more than once in your life, "Oh, I'm sorry, I don't work here, I'm just shopping."

Authentic energy enhances our ability to connect with people more readily. Again, we now have science to support this claim. Heart Math, a company that conducts research on stress and well-being, has measured the electrical energy of the human heart. This energy can be measured from 1500 feet away (heartmath.com). Imagine how magnified the energy of a dynamic personality must be, particularly when it is the appreciative kind. Regardless of your personality type, the ability to convey your vitality to others will bring more opportunities your way. People are more drawn to you. Some experts even go so far as to say that confident people are capable of generating more ideas and making better decisions.

From a career advancement perspective, and my own utterly unscientific research, I have found genuine energy, the kind that says "I want to be here" and "I am interested in you" can be the difference between staying stuck or moving forward. It's like currency that you can accumulate and then use as tender when opportunity knocks.

Where Does Your Inspiration Come From?

Whether or not we care to admit it, we are influenced by the people closest to us – family, friends, colleagues, to name a few. Directly and indirectly, they can have an effect on our decision-making, what we focus on, what we care about, even our outlook on life. Motivational speaker Jim Rohn is credited for encapsulating this concept into what he calls the Average of Five: we are the average of the five people we spend the most time with.[28]

As we begin wrapping up our confidence-building journey, it might be helpful – no, that was mitigated speech – it *will* be helpful to take an inventory of who is in your life and what role they serve. Sometimes we hang on to friends, co-workers, and loved ones out of a sense of loyalty or responsibility. That may be a legitimate reason, but have you thought about it enough to know that it really is necessary to keep those people in your circle? The only way to achieve a consistently confident mindset is to figure out who in your life keeps you motivated and even happy; and who in your life is dragging you down.

Are you keeping good company? Do your friends and family support your goals and admire your achievements or are they holding you back? Do your co-workers acknowledge your skills and contributions in a way that allows you to make a meaningful contribution and even develop new skills? Or do they subtly or not-so-subtly block your progress? As one of my clients said after completing the exercise on the next page, "I never realized how much of a negative force my friend Angie is in my life. That's not exactly true. What I meant to say was that up until this moment, I hadn't allowed myself to admit it, especially out loud to another person. I've known her for 15 years and I think she stopped being a good friend five years ago."

Change is hard enough without having to add the burden of severing ties with the people in our inner circle. But think of the alternative: a life in which you never reach your true potential, never find your passion, and never take risks. Psychologist Kurt Lewin is known as the founder of group dynamics and social psychology. His best-known theory of human behavior states that it is "related both to one's personal characteristics and to the social situation in which one finds oneself."[30] Lewin's change research is a three-part model: unfreezing/change/refreezing. In order to change, there must be a driving force – an upset in the status quo that then results in a change. Driving forces must be stronger than restraining forces in order for change to occur.

On the next page you will have the opportunity to decide whether the driving force needed in your life right now is to move someone out of your inner circle. You might also discover that your driving force is the renewed confidence you feel as a result of knowing that your five people are truly sources of inspiration and support.

Coaching Session

Take some time right now to reflect on who is in your life and whether or not they provide the inspiration, support, challenge, and motivation you need to access the get-up-and-go kind of energy to achieve your goals. Who are the five people in *your* life? Who do you spend the most time with? Write their names down in the left-hand column. Then in right-hand column, write down a few adjectives that best describe them and how they relate to you, how they influence you, possibly even their outlook on life.

Name of Person	Descriptors
1.	
2.	
3.	
4.	
5.	

Should they stay or should they go? Are they helping you grow, feel challenged, and supported? Or are they keeping you stuck?

If you recognized yourself in any of the examples provided in this book, then be sure to complete the final coaching session. It is designed to help you summon all the positive and meaningful aspects of who you are and how you show up in the world. With that awareness comes the gift of self-respect. With self-respect comes the confidence to keep your head up and yours ears tuned to possibilities. Lack of confidence comes with blinders and ear muffs. True confidence comes with radar, antennas, and transmitters.

Final Coaching Session

The most important question I will ask of you is right here:

What inspires you...

about <u>you</u>?

Write it down. Be bold, be thorough, and be explicit. Then say it out loud so you can hear it come out of your mouth. I know, I've asked that of you before, but it's important. Remember the story about rehearsing in your head. It's not the same as hearing your words spoken by your own voice.

If you feel your impetus to take action has increased as a result of reading this book, perhaps you will decide right now to share your response with someone whose opinion you respect and ask for their feedback. Who knows, you might have overlooked an important quality that can be added to your answer.

What inspires me about me is...

_____

_____

_____

_____

_____

_____

"You could say I'd never had a true religious moment, the kind where you
[are] spoken to by a voice that seems other than yourself,
spoken to so genuinely you see the words shining on trees and clouds.
But I had such a moment right then, standing in my own ordinary room
I heard a voice say, Lily Melissa Owens, your jar is open."

- The Secret Life of Bees by Sue Monk Kidd

Let me leave you with my personal definition of confidence:

Feeling *really* good about
being yourself in *any* situation.

Remember, motivation lasts about 14 days. The final phase of this journey involves making a commitment to spend more energy and effort taking action toward achieving your goals, and less time seeking approval of who you are or what you want. Starting today with one specific action is the best first step. Letting a few days go by before taking any action is the least effective option.

Thank you for investing in this book – I hope you now see that it was an investment in yourself. One more thing before we say good-bye. I've created a Confidence Pledge which I hope will come in handy whenever the weedy fingers of self-doubt creep back into your consciousness. Recite the pledge as a way of renewing your commitment to feeling consistently and genuinely confident:

*I will embrace the positive energy
that comes from true confidence
and release the demons
of fear, doubt and insecurity.
If they do find a way to sneak back in
I will zap them with a generous dose of
humor and loving kindness.*

references

1.   *Ambition and Gender at Work,* Institute for Leadership and Management, February, 2011.

2.   *Unlocking the Full Potential of Women in the U. S. Economy*, Joanna Barsh, Lorena Yee, McKinsey & Co., April, 2011.

3.   *The Benefit of Power Posing Before a High-Stakes Social Evaluation*, Cuddy, Amy J.C., Caroline A. Wilmuth, and Dana R. Carney, Harvard Business School Working Paper, 2012.

4.   *Outliers: The Story of Success*, Malcolm Gladwell, Little Brown, New York, 2008.

5.   *The Secret Life of Pronouns: What Our Words Say About Us*, James Pennebaker, 2011.

6.   *The Hidden Power of Backstories* in Tell to Win, Peter Gruber, Crown Publishing, 2011.

7.   *Silent Messages*, Albert Mehrabian, Wadsworth Publishing, 1971.

8.   *Seven Careers in a Lifetime? Think Twice*, Numbers Guy Blog, Wall Street Journal, 2010.

9.   *Four Stages for Learning Any New Skill*, Noel Burch, Gordon Training International, 1970.

10. *Flourish: A Visionary New Understanding of Happiness and Well-being*, Martin Seligman, Free Press, 2011.

11. *Emotional Intelligence: Why it Can Matter More Thank IQ*, Daniel Goleman, Bantam, 2006.

12. *Furious Serena Williams Dumped Out of U.S. Open*, David Gardner, dailymail.com, 2009.

13. *Brain Scans Show Distinctive Patterns in People with Generalized Anxiety Disorder,* Science Daily, 2009.

14. *"Mayhem and Foolishness"* – thank you Niecy Nash, Clean House, Style Network, 2009.

15. *Getting Unstuck*, Pema Chodron, Sounds True, 2004.

16. R.H. Bruskin Associates research findings, 1973.

17. *The Actor's Vow,* Elia Kazan, 1909-2003.

18. *The Perfect Candidate*, NACE Job Outlook, 2008.

19. *A Theory of Human Motivation*, Abraham Maslow, Psychological Review, 1943.

20. *Communication Mosaics*, Julia T. Wood, Wadsworth, Cengage Learning, 2008.

21. *The Art of Extempore Speaking*, Louis Bautain, McDevitt-Wilson's, Inc, 1916.

22. *The Art of Woo: Using Strategic Persuasion to Sell Your Ideas*, Richard Shell, Mario Moussa, Penguin Group, 2007.

23. *Influence: The Psychology of Persuasion*, Harper Collins, 2006.

24. *Beautiful Evidence,* Edward Tufte, Graphics Press, 2006.

25. A Brand Called You, Tom Peters, Fast Company, 1997.

26. *Resonate: Present Visual Stories That Transform Audiences*, Nancy Duarte, John Wiley & Sons, 2010.

27. *Five Steps to Developing Your Leadership Brand*, Dave Ulrich, Norm Smallwood, Harvard Management Newsletter, Harvard Management Update, 2007.

28. *The Art of Exceptional Living*, Jim Rohn, Nightingale Conant.

29. *Acting On Stage and Off*, Robert Barton, Wadsworth, Cengage, 2009.

30. *Defining the "Field at a Given Time,"* Kurt Lewin, *Psychological Review,* 1943.

appendix

Reading Aloud Exercise
Totally like whatever, you know?
by Taylor Mali

In case you hadn't noticed,
it has somehow become uncool
to sound like you know what you're talking about?
Or believe strongly in what you're saying?
Invisible question marks and parenthetical (you know?)'s
have been attaching themselves to the ends of our sentences
Even when those sentences aren't, like, questions. You know?

Declarative sentences, so-called
because they used to, like, DECLARE things to be true, okay,
as opposed to other things are, like, totally, you know, not—
have been infected by a totally hip and tragically cool interrogative tone? You know?
Like, don't think I'm uncool just because I've noticed this;
this is just like the word on the street, you know?
It's like what I've heard? I have nothing personally invested in my own opinions, okay?
I'm just inviting you to join me in my uncertainty?

What has happened to our conviction?
Where are the limbs out on which we once walked?
Have they been, like, chopped down with the rest of the rain forest?
Or do we have, like, nothing to say?
Has society become so, like, totally . . .
I mean absolutely . . . You know?
That we've just gotten to the point where it's just, like . . . whatever!

And so actually our disarticulation . . . ness
is just a clever sort of . . . thing
to disguise the fact that we've become
the most aggressively inarticulate generation to come along since . . .
you know, a long, long time ago!

I entreat you, I implore you, I exhort you,
I challenge you: To speak with conviction.

To say what you believe in a manner that bespeaks
the determination with which you believe it.
Because contrary to the wisdom of the bumper sticker,
it is not enough these days to simply QUESTION AUTHORITY.
You have to speak with it, too.

For more poems by Taylor Mali, visit www.taylormali.com